Table of Contents

 W9-AWU-236

Introduction 5

Unit 1 Numbers 7

1.NBT.1	Lesson 1	Numbers 8
1.NBT.1	Lesson 2	Counting 12
1.NBT.2.a, b	Lesson 3	Place Value 16
1.NBT.2.c	Lesson 4	More Place Value 20
1.NBT.3	Lesson 5	Comparing Numbers 24
	Review	Numbers 28

Unit 2 Understanding Addition and Subtraction 31

1.OA.5	Lesson 1	Counting to Add and Subtract 32
1.OA.6	Lesson 2	Addition and Subtraction Strategies 36
1.OA.6	Lesson 3	More Addition and Subtraction Strategies 40
1.OA.3	Lesson 4	Properties of Operations 44
	Review	Understanding Addition and Subtraction 48

Unit 3 Addition 51

1.NBT.4, 1.NBT.5	Lesson 1	Adding 10 52
1.NBT.4	Lesson 2	Adding Numbers 56
1.OA.1, 1.OA.2	Lesson 3	Addition Word Problems 60
	Review	Addition 64

Unit 4 Subtraction 67

1.NBT.5	Lesson 1	Subtracting 10 68
1.NBT.6, 1.OA.4	Lesson 2	Subtracting Numbers 72
1.OA.1	Lesson 3	Subtraction Word Problems 76
	Review	Subtraction 80

Unit 5 Number Sentences 83

1.OA.7	Lesson 1	Understanding Number Sentences 84
1.OA.8	Lesson 2	Solving Number Sentences 88
	Review	Number Sentences 92

Unit 6 Measurement...95

    1.MD.1   Lesson 1   Comparing and Ordering Length.........................96

    1.MD.2   Lesson 2   Finding Length 100

    1.MD.3   Lesson 3   Time 104

               Review   Measurement 108

Unit 7 Data Displays 111

    1.MD.4   Lesson 1   Tables 112

    1.MD.4   Lesson 2   Tally Charts 116

    1.MD.4   Lesson 3   Bar Graphs 120

    1.MD.4   Lesson 4   Picture Graphs 124

               Review   Data Displays 128

Unit 8 Geometry 131

    1.G.1   Lesson 1   Flat Shapes 132

    1.G.1   Lesson 2   Solid Shapes 136

    1.G.2   Lesson 3   Putting Shapes Together 140

    1.G.3   Lesson 4   Making Equal Parts................................ 144

               Review   Geometry..148

Practice Test 151

Glossary 167

Mathematics
for the Common Core State Standards

GRADE 1

ISBN 978-0-8454-6909-5

Copyright © 2011 The Continental Press, Inc.

No part of this publication may be reproduced in any form or by any means, electronic, mechanical, photocopying, recording, or otherwise, without the prior written permission of the publisher. All rights reserved. Printed in the United States of America.

Welcome to Finish Line Mathematics for the Common Core State Standards

About This Book

Finish Line Mathematics for the Common Core State Standards will help you get ready for math tests. You are learning new math skills. This book helps you with the most important ones. You learn new things each year. You need to really understand the ideas you learn. They help you as you learn more and more.

This book has units of lessons. Each lesson talks about one main math idea. You have already learned these ideas. The lesson helps you remember them.

There are practice problems, too. You have done these kinds of problems before. There are multiple-choice problems. Each problem has four answers. You must pick the best one. One of the problems is done for you. You can read about the correct answer.

There are constructed-response problems. You have to write the answer. Sometimes you have to show your work. Sometimes you have to tell what you did. This shows if you know how to do the problem. One of the problems is done for you. You can read about the correct answer.

There are extended-response problems. These problems have two parts. Write your answers. This problem gives you a clue.

Each unit has a review. You will use all the ideas. You will do all the types of problems.

There is a practice test. It is at the end of the book. You will use everything you practiced. There is a glossary, too. It is a list of important words. It tells you what the words mean. You might forget what a word means. You can check here for help.

© The Continental Press, Inc.   DUPLICATING THIS MATERIAL IS ILLEGAL.

The Goals of Learning Math

You use math a lot. Sometimes you think about it. Sometimes you do not think about it.

You want to be good at math. You need good habits. A habit is the way you do something. And you need good thoughts about math.

- Read problems carefully. Make a plan. Do not give up. Your plan might not work. Try again!

- Look for math around you. Look for ways you use math when you are not in school.

- Think of ideas. Tell why your idea is correct. Think about other people's ideas. Ask questions to help you understand.

- Use math models. Draw pictures. Use number blocks. Make a number line.

- Use math tools. Tools help you find the answer.

- Be careful with your work. Write neatly. Mark your answer. Use good words to tell what you did.

- Think about things you already know. Use them to learn new things.

- Look for patterns. You might be able to find new ways of doing something.

Practice these habits. They can help you remember ideas. They can help you learn new ideas. Then math will be easier to do. You will want to use it all of the time!

© The Continental Press, Inc.   DUPLICATING THIS MATERIAL IS ILLEGAL.

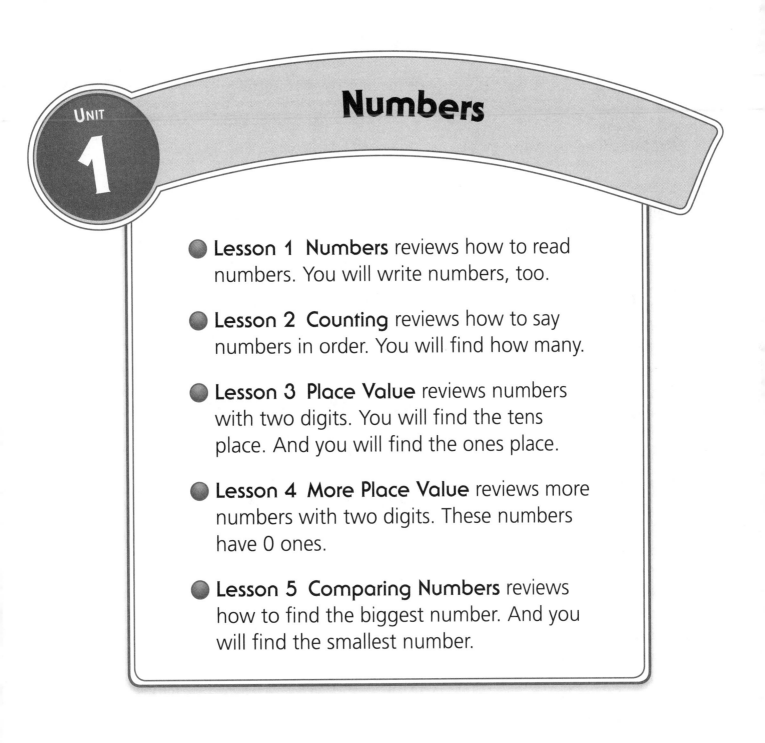

Numbers

UNIT 1

● **Lesson 1 Numbers** reviews how to read numbers. You will write numbers, too.

● **Lesson 2 Counting** reviews how to say numbers in order. You will find how many.

● **Lesson 3 Place Value** reviews numbers with two digits. You will find the tens place. And you will find the ones place.

● **Lesson 4 More Place Value** reviews more numbers with two digits. These numbers have 0 ones.

● **Lesson 5 Comparing Numbers** reviews how to find the biggest number. And you will find the smallest number.

© The Continental Press, Inc.   DUPLICATING THIS MATERIAL IS ILLEGAL.

Numbers

1.NBT.1

🏁 Here are some more numbers:

11 eleven
12 twelve
13 thirteen
14 fourteen
15 fifteen
16 sixteen
17 seventeen
18 eighteen
19 nineteen
20 twenty

30 thirty
40 forty
50 fifty
60 sixty
70 seventy
80 eighty
90 ninety
100 one hundred
110 one hundred ten
120 one hundred twenty

Some numbers have more than one **digit.**

52

This number has two digits: 5 and 2.

Numbers tell how many. You use numbers to count. You can write numbers. And you can read numbers.

You can write numbers in different ways.

How many crayons are there?

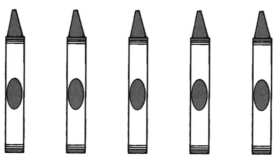

There are 5 crayons. The word for 5 is five.

Jim has eight balls. What number is eight?

Write the number for eight: 8

These are the numbers from zero to ten.

0	1	2	3	4	5
zero	one	two	three	four	five

6	7	8	9	10
six	seven	eight	nine	ten

© The Continental Press, Inc.   DUPLICATING THIS MATERIAL IS ILLEGAL.

SAMPLE How many hats are there?

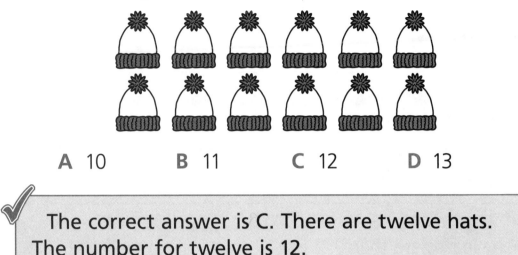

A 10   B 11   C 12   D 13

The correct answer is C. There are twelve hats.
The number for twelve is 12.

1 How do you write 86 with words?

A eight-six

B eighty-six

C eighty-sixty

D eighty-nine

2 Which number is twenty-five?

A 25

B 205

C 35

D 52

3 How many spoons are there?

A three

B four

C five

D six

4 Which words mean 43?

A four three

B three four

C forty-three

D thirty-four

© The Continental Press, Inc.   DUPLICATING THIS MATERIAL IS ILLEGAL.

SAMPLE How do you write 71 with words?

Answer _____

✓
There are two digits in the number. The first one is a 7. The second one is a 1. The first number means seventy. The second number means one. So 71 is seventy-one.

5 How many leaves are there?

Write the number. Write the word name.

Number _____

Word name _____

6 Write the number for ninety-six.

Answer _____

7 Write the words for 32.

Answer _____

© The Continental Press, Inc.   DUPLICATING THIS MATERIAL IS ILLEGAL.

8 Liz picked these flowers.

Part A Write the number of flowers.

Answer _____

Part B Liz said she picked eighteen flowers. Is Liz correct? Tell how you know.

Look at the number in part A. How do you write this number with words?

_____

_____

_____

_____

_____

© The Continental Press, Inc.   DUPLICATING THIS MATERIAL IS ILLEGAL.

Counting

1.NBT.1

Count to find how many in a group. Always start with 1 to count this way.

Use numbers to count. Say numbers in order when you **count.** Count to find how many.

Count the number of fish. Write each number.

Point to the green fish. Say the number 1.

Point to the white fish. Say the number 2.

Point to the gray fish. Say the number 3.

There are 3 fish. Count: 1, 2, 3

Count to write numbers in order. You do not need to start with 1. You can start with any number. Then count up.

Count to find the number that comes after. The number after is 1 more.

What number comes after 50?

Count up one from 50. This is the number after: 51

A **number line** shows numbers in order.

A number line can start with any number. It can end with any number.

What number is missing?

50 51 52 53 54 55 ☐ 57 58 59 60

The missing number is between two numbers.

Look at the number before it: 55

Look at the number after it: 57

The missing number is 56.

© The Continental Press, Inc.   DUPLICATING THIS MATERIAL IS ILLEGAL.

SAMPLE Rosa starts with 7. She counts to 12. What numbers does she say?

A 7, 12   **C** 7, 8, 9, 12

B 7, 6, 5, 12   **D** 7, 8, 9, 10, 11, 12

The correct answer is D. Start with 7. Count up by ones. Stop when you get to 12: 7, 8, 9, 10, 11, 12.

1 Look at this number line.

70 71 72 73 74 75 76 ☐ 78 79 80

What number is missing?

A 67   **C** 77

B 75   **D** 86

2 Julia counted 5 circles. Which group did Julia count?

A ○○○○

B ○○○○○

C ○○○○○○

D ○○○○○○○

3 Pedro counted these pears.

How many pears did he count?

A 9   **C** 7

B 8   **D** 6

4 What two numbers are missing?

12 13 ☐ 15 16 17 18 19 20 ☐ 22

A 15 and 17   **C** 14 and 20

B 13 and 14   **D** 14 and 21

5 Ming starts at 45. She counts to 48. What numbers does she say?

A 45, 46, 47, 48

B 45, 46, 48

C 45, 46, 48, 49

D 56, 57, 58

© The Continental Press, Inc. DUPLICATING THIS MATERIAL IS ILLEGAL.

SAMPLE Count this group of triangles. Write each number.

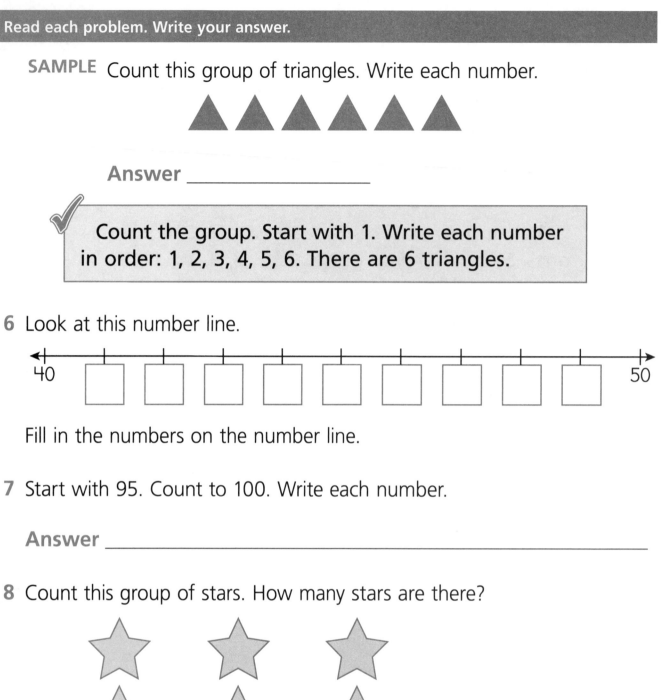

Answer _____

✓ Count the group. Start with 1. Write each number in order: 1, 2, 3, 4, 5, 6. There are 6 triangles.

6 Look at this number line.

40 ☐ ☐ ☐ ☐ ☐ ☐ ☐ ☐ ☐ 50

Fill in the numbers on the number line.

7 Start with 95. Count to 100. Write each number.

Answer _____

8 Count this group of stars. How many stars are there?

Answer _____

© The Continental Press, Inc.   DUPLICATING THIS MATERIAL IS ILLEGAL.

9 Nina counted this group of blocks.

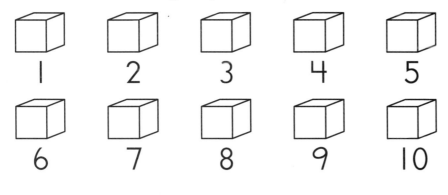

Part A Nina gets one more block. What number will she say to count this block?

What number comes after 10?

Answer _____

Part B Nina gets some more blocks. She wants to count all her blocks. Write the numbers under these blocks. Start with the number after 10.

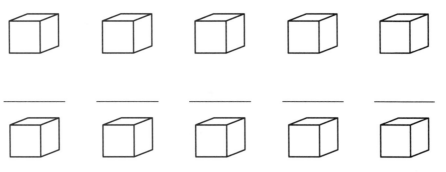

How many blocks does Nina have in all?

Answer _____

© The Continental Press, Inc.   DUPLICATING THIS MATERIAL IS ILLEGAL.

Place Value

1.NBT.2.a, b

A ten is made up of 10 ones.

You can group numbers as tens and ones.

What is this number?

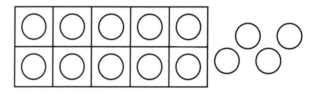

Count the tens: 1

Count the ones: 4

The number has 1 ten and 4 ones: 14

The number is 14.

Tens and ones are places in a number.

What number is 1 ten 7 ones?

Tens	Ones
1	7

The tens are on the left.

The ones are on the right.

This number is 17.

The tens are on the left. The ones are on the right.

14
↑ ↑
Tens Ones

The **place value** tells what number is in each place.

Models can help you show place value.

= 10

□ = 1

© The Continental Press, Inc.   DUPLICATING THIS MATERIAL IS ILLEGAL.

SAMPLE Which of these is 1 ten 8 ones?

A 108 **B** 18 **C** 81 **D** 801

> The correct answer is B. The tens are on the left. The ones are on the right. The number is 18.

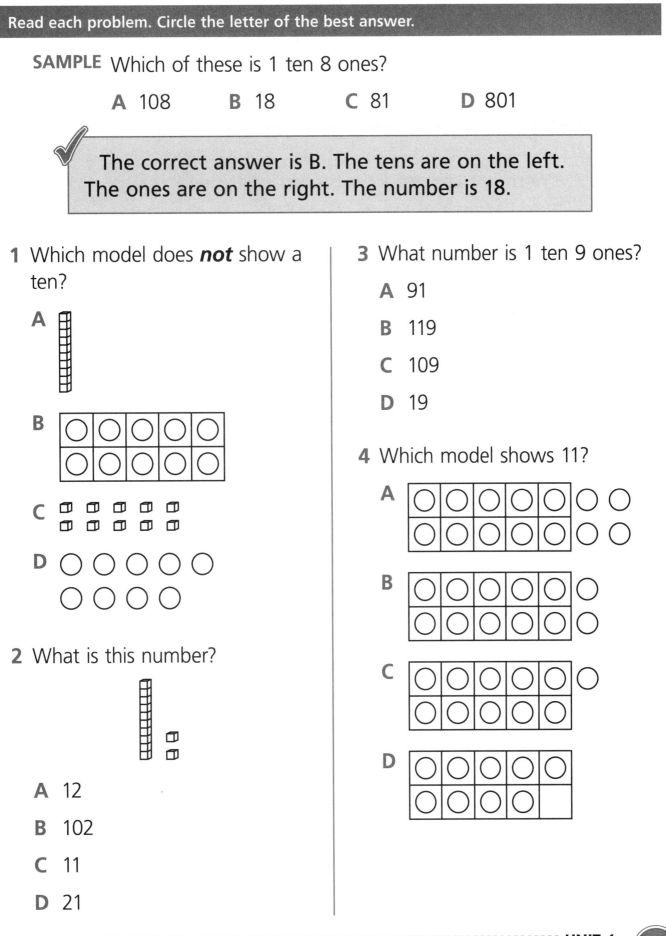

1 Which model does **not** show a ten?

A

B

C

D

2 What is this number?

A 12

B 102

C 11

D 21

3 What number is 1 ten 9 ones?

A 91

B 119

C 109

D 19

4 Which model shows 11?

A

B

C

D

© The Continental Press, Inc. DUPLICATING THIS MATERIAL IS ILLEGAL.

SAMPLE What is the number at the right?

Answer _____

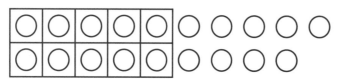

✓ There is 1 tens rod. So the number has 1 ten.
There are 5 ones cubes. The number has 5 ones.
The number is 1 ten 5 ones, or 15.

5 Write the number of tens and ones.

Tens _____

Ones _____

6 What is the number in problem 5?

Answer _____

7 Draw a model to show a ten.

8 What number is 1 ten 3 ones?

Answer _____

© The Continental Press, Inc. DUPLICATING THIS MATERIAL IS ILLEGAL.

9 Mrs. Smith has these forks.

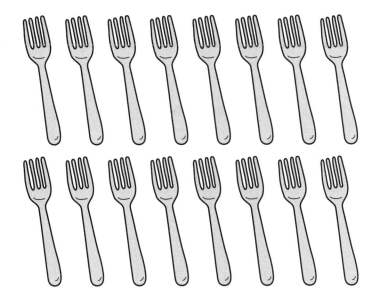

Part A Circle a ten in the group above.

Part B Write the number of forks. Tell how you found the number.

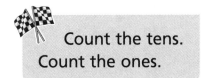
Count the tens.
Count the ones.

_____

_____

_____

_____

© The Continental Press, Inc.   DUPLICATING THIS MATERIAL IS ILLEGAL.

More Place Value

1.NBT.2.c

There are special names for groups of ten.

10	ten
20	twenty
30	thirty
40	forty
50	fifty
60	sixty
70	seventy
80	eighty
90	ninety

Always write the 0 in the ones place.

4 is not the same as 40.

Some numbers have only tens. They have no ones.

What is this number?

Count the tens: 4

Count the ones: 0

Name the number: 40

This number is 40. The word for 40 is forty.

Show the number in a table. Show the number of tens. Show the number of ones.

Tens	Ones
4	0

This table shows 40.

© The Continental Press, Inc.   DUPLICATING THIS MATERIAL IS ILLEGAL.

SAMPLE What is this number?

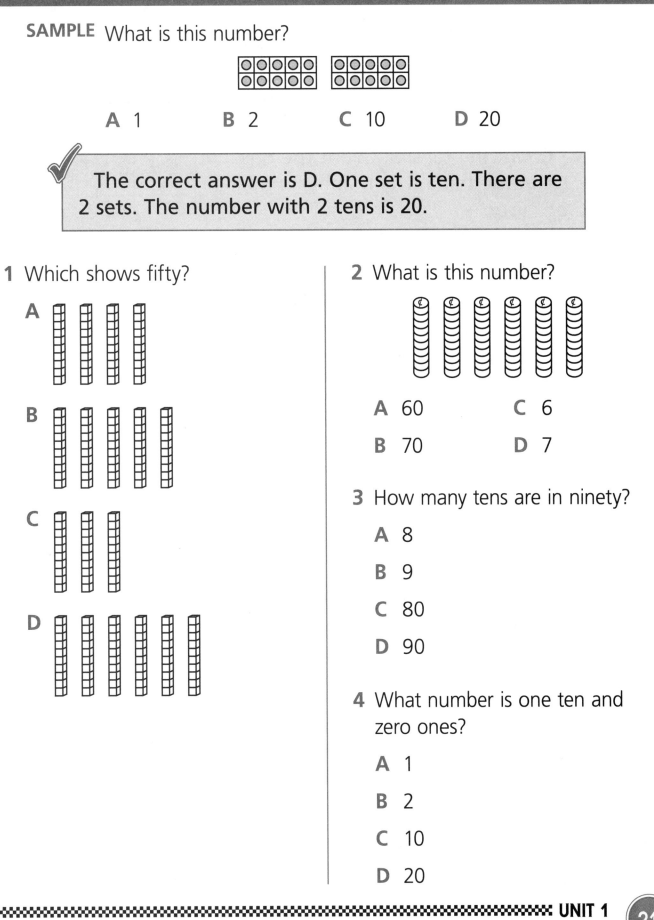

A 1 **B** 2 **C** 10 **D** 20

✓ The correct answer is D. One set is ten. There are 2 sets. The number with 2 tens is 20.

1 Which shows fifty?

A

B

C

D

2 What is this number?

A 60 **C** 6

B 70 **D** 7

3 How many tens are in ninety?

A 8

B 9

C 80

D 90

4 What number is one ten and zero ones?

A 1

B 2

C 10

D 20

© The Continental Press, Inc. DUPLICATING THIS MATERIAL IS ILLEGAL.

SAMPLE Look at the model. Write the tens and ones in the table.

Tens	Ones

✓ Count the tens: 3. Count the ones: 0. Fill in the table. The number is 30, or thirty.

Tens	Ones
3	0

5 Write the number of tens. Write the number.

Tens _____

Number _____

6 Look at the model. Write the number of tens and ones in the table.

Tens	Ones

7 Read the number.

sixty

Write the number of tens. Write the number of ones.

Tens _____

Ones _____

© The Continental Press, Inc.   DUPLICATING THIS MATERIAL IS ILLEGAL.

8 Mike made stacks of pennies.

Part A How many tens did Mike make?

Answer _____

How many pennies are in one stack?

Part B A penny is 1 cent. How many cents does Mike have? Tell how you know.

_____

_____

_____

_____

© The Continental Press, Inc.   DUPLICATING THIS MATERIAL IS ILLEGAL.

Comparing Numbers

LESSON 5

1.NBT.3

Compare the digits. First look at the tens. Then look at the ones.

Tens	Ones
3	7

The > and < symbols point to the smaller number.

> mean "is greater than."

58 > 37

< means "is less than."

37 < 58

The = symbol means "is equal to." **Equal** means "the same as."

24 = 24

You can **compare** numbers.

Which number is **greater:** 37 or 54?

Find how many tens and ones.

37 is 3 tens and 7 ones

58 is 5 tens and 8 ones

Compare the tens. 5 tens is more than 3 tens.

58 is greater than 37.

You can use symbols to compare. The > **symbol** means "is greater than." The < **symbol** means "is less than."

Which number is **less:** 23 or 21?

Find how many tens and ones.

23 is 2 tens and 3 ones

21 is 2 tens and 1 one

Both number have 2 tens. Compare the ones. 1 one is less than 3 ones.

21 is less than 23.

Use the < symbol: 21 < 23

© The Continental Press, Inc.   DUPLICATING THIS MATERIAL IS ILLEGAL.

SAMPLE Which number is greater than 87?

A 78   B 81   C 87   D 90

✓ The correct answer is D. 87 is 8 tens and 7 ones. Compare the tens. 90 is 9 tens and 0 ones. 9 tens is more than 8 tens. So 90 is greater than 87.

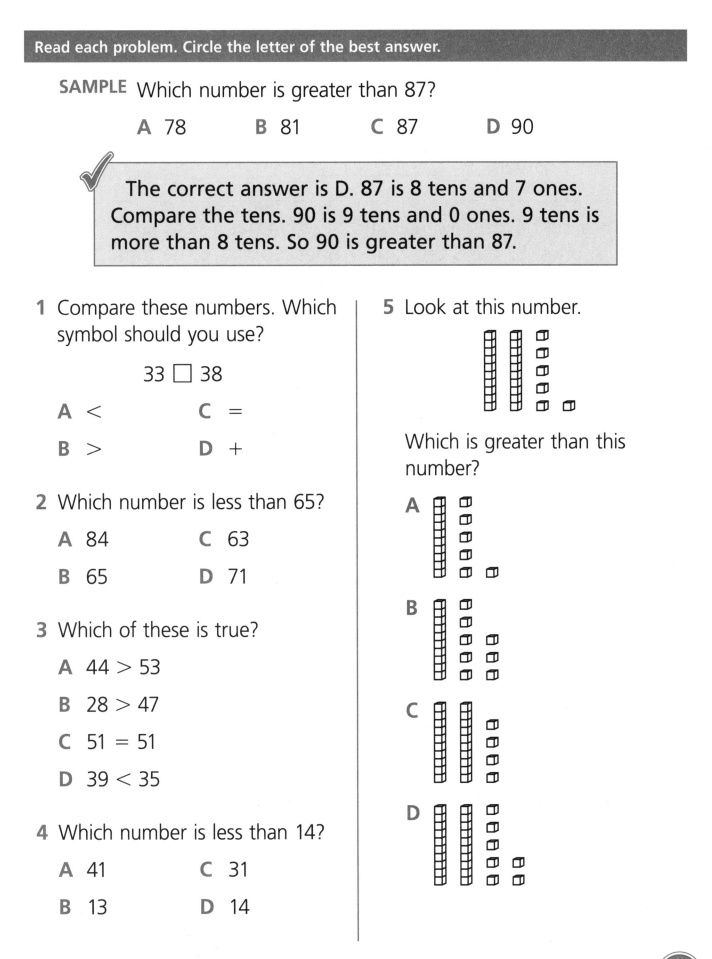

1 Compare these numbers. Which symbol should you use?

33 ☐ 38

A <   C =

B >   D +

2 Which number is less than 65?

A 84   C 63

B 65   D 71

3 Which of these is true?

A 44 > 53

B 28 > 47

C 51 = 51

D 39 < 35

4 Which number is less than 14?

A 41   C 31

B 13   D 14

5 Look at this number.

Which is greater than this number?

A

B

C

D

© The Continental Press, Inc.   DUPLICATING THIS MATERIAL IS ILLEGAL.

SAMPLE Kate has 74 flowers. Li has 57 flowers. Who has fewer flowers?

Answer _____

✓ Find how many tens and ones. 74 has 7 tens and 4 ones. 57 has 5 tens and 7 ones. Compare the tens. 5 tens is less than 7 tens. So 57 is less than 74. Li has fewer flowers.

6 Use <, >, or = to compare. Write the symbol in the box.

7 Tim compared two numbers. He wrote 24 > 42. Is Tim correct? Tell how you know.

_____

_____

_____

8 Write a number that is greater than 67. Write a number that is less than 67.

Greater than _____

Less than _____

© The Continental Press, Inc. DUPLICATING THIS MATERIAL IS ILLEGAL.

9 Nobu has these two numbers.

Tens	Ones

Tens	Ones

Part A Write the number of tens and ones above.
Compare the numbers. Use >, <, or =.

Answer _____

Part B Look at the number on the right. Nobu
took away one tens rod. Compare the
numbers now. Use >, <, or =. Tell how
you know.

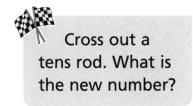

Cross out a
tens rod. What is
the new number?

_____

_____

_____

_____

_____

© The Continental Press, Inc.   DUPLICATING THIS MATERIAL IS ILLEGAL.

REVIEW

Numbers

Read each problem. Circle the letter of the best answer.

1 How many lollipops are there?

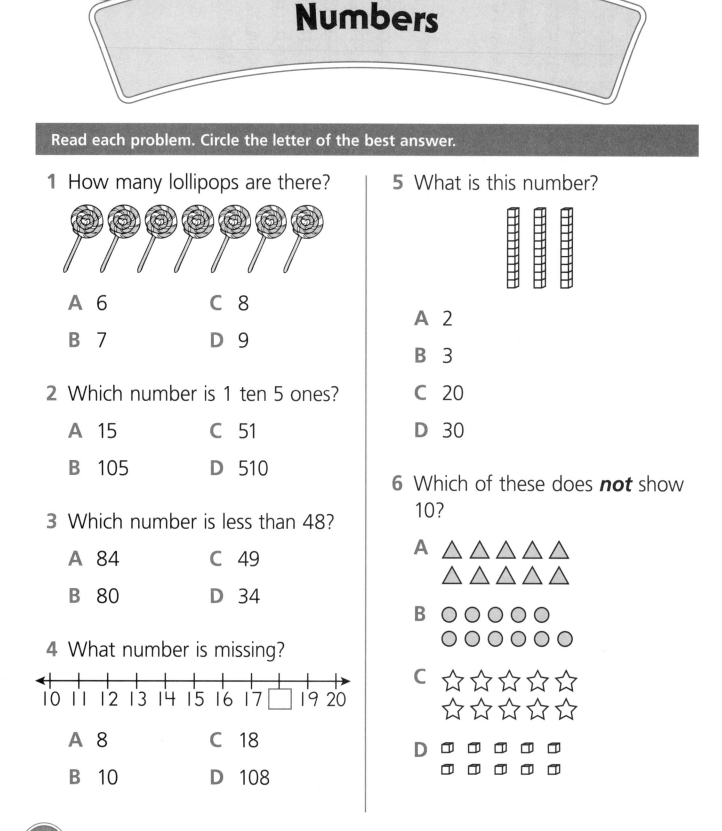

A 6   **C** 8

B 7   **D** 9

2 Which number is 1 ten 5 ones?

A 15   **C** 51

B 105   **D** 510

3 Which number is less than 48?

A 84   **C** 49

B 80   **D** 34

4 What number is missing?

10 11 12 13 14 15 16 17 ☐ 19 20

A 8   **C** 18

B 10   **D** 108

5 What is this number?

A 2

B 3

C 20

D 30

6 Which of these does **not** show 10?

A △△△△△ △△△△

B ○○○○○ ○○○○○

C ☆☆☆☆☆ ☆☆☆☆☆

D ▱▱▱▱▱ ▱▱▱▱▱

© The Continental Press, Inc. DUPLICATING THIS MATERIAL IS ILLEGAL.

7 Count this group of balloons. Write each number.

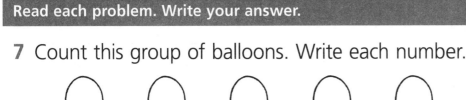

_____   _____   _____   _____   _____

8 Write the number for seventy-four.

Answer _____

9 Write the number of tens and ones. What is the number?

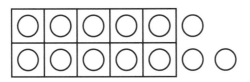

Tens _____

Ones _____

Number _____

10 Use <, >, or = to compare. Write the symbol in the box.

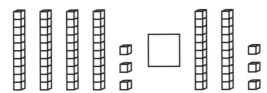

© The Continental Press, Inc.   DUPLICATING THIS MATERIAL IS ILLEGAL.

11 Look at the model at the right.

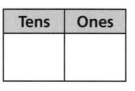

Part A Write the number of tens. Write the number of ones. What is the number?

Tens	Ones

Answer _____

Part B Look at your number in part A. Write a number that is greater. Tell how you know.

_____

_____

_____

_____

12 Look at the number line.

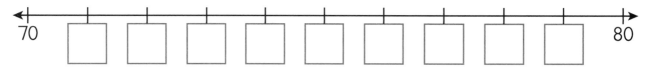

Part A Look at the two numbers on the number line. Write the word names.

70 _____

80 _____

Part B Write the missing numbers on the number line.

© The Continental Press, Inc.   DUPLICATING THIS MATERIAL IS ILLEGAL.

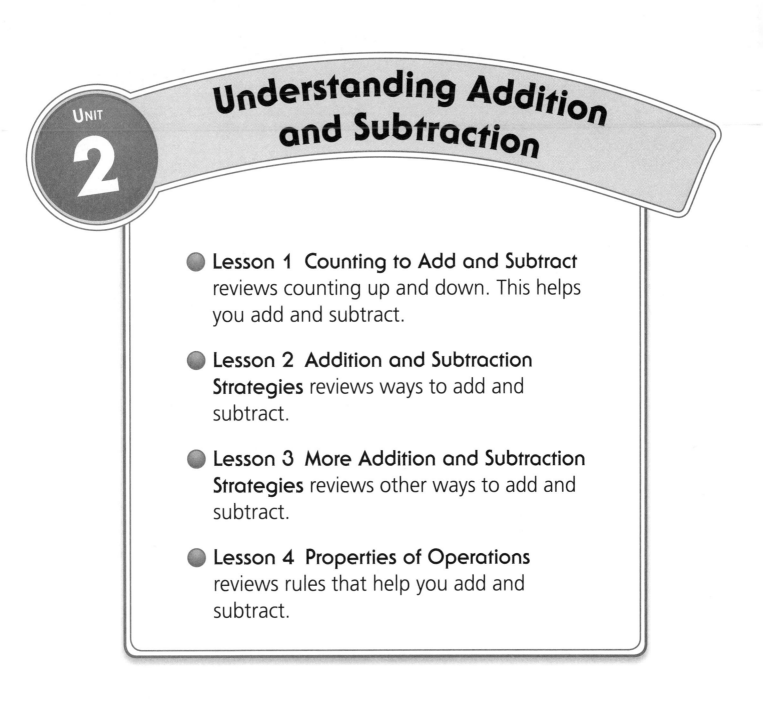

Understanding Addition and Subtraction

UNIT 2

- **Lesson 1 Counting to Add and Subtract** reviews counting up and down. This helps you add and subtract.

- **Lesson 2 Addition and Subtraction Strategies** reviews ways to add and subtract.

- **Lesson 3 More Addition and Subtraction Strategies** reviews other ways to add and subtract.

- **Lesson 4 Properties of Operations** reviews rules that help you add and subtract.

© The Continental Press, Inc.   DUPLICATING THIS MATERIAL IS ILLEGAL.

LESSON 1

Counting to Add and Subtract

1.OA.5

🏁

Count up to add.

Always start with the greater number. Then you do not need to count as many.

You can **count on** to **add.** Start with the bigger number. Then count on.

There are 6 apples.
Kim gets 2 more.
How many in all?

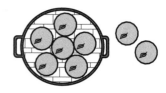

6 is more than 2. Start with 6. Count up: 7, 8

There are 8 apples in all.

Count back to subtract.

You can **count back** to **subtract.** Start with the bigger number. Count back.

There are 5 birds. 1 flies away. How many are left?

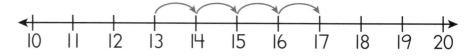

5 is more than 1. Start with 5. Count back 1: 4

There are 4 birds left.

A number line can start with any number. It can end with any number.

A number line can help you add and subtract.

Juan has 13 stamps. He gets 4 more. How many in all?

Find 13 on the number line. Count up 4.

Juan has 17 stamps in all.

© The Continental Press, Inc.   DUPLICATING THIS MATERIAL IS ILLEGAL.

SAMPLE Count on two more from 12. What numbers do you say?

A 11, 10 **B** 12, 13 **C** 13, 15 **D** 13, 14

The correct answer is D. Start with 12. Count on two more: 13, 14.

Use the number line to answer questions 1–4.

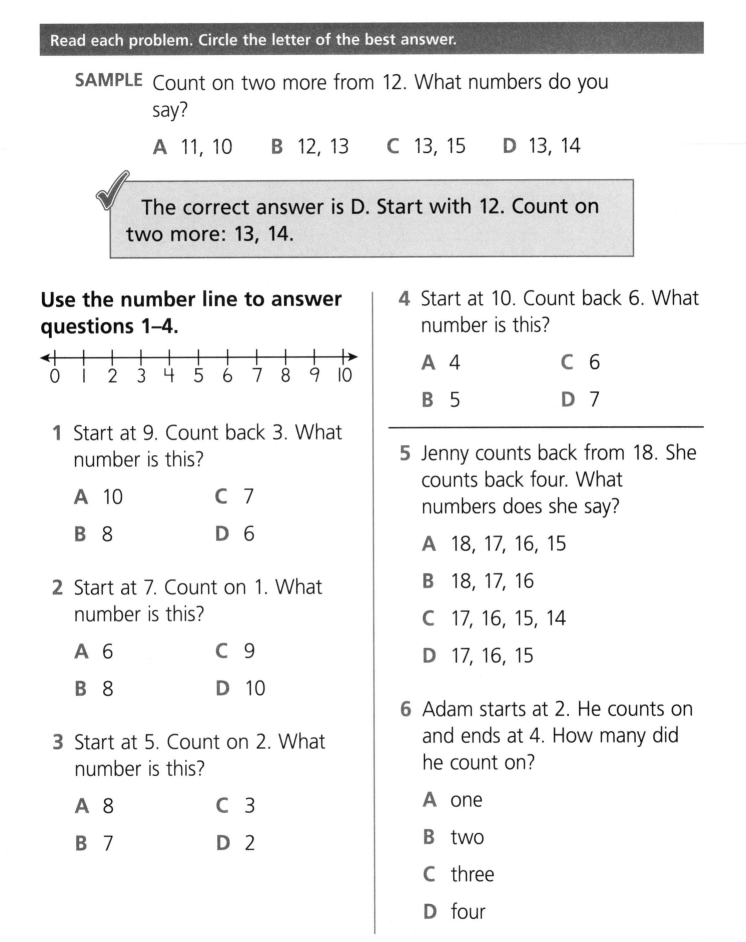

1 Start at 9. Count back 3. What number is this?

A 10 **C** 7

B 8 **D** 6

2 Start at 7. Count on 1. What number is this?

A 6 **C** 9

B 8 **D** 10

3 Start at 5. Count on 2. What number is this?

A 8 **C** 3

B 7 **D** 2

4 Start at 10. Count back 6. What number is this?

A 4 **C** 6

B 5 **D** 7

5 Jenny counts back from 18. She counts back four. What numbers does she say?

A 18, 17, 16, 15

B 18, 17, 16

C 17, 16, 15, 14

D 17, 16, 15

6 Adam starts at 2. He counts on and ends at 4. How many did he count on?

A one

B two

C three

D four

© The Continental Press, Inc. DUPLICATING THIS MATERIAL IS ILLEGAL.

SAMPLE Hyo counts back to subtract. He subtracts 6 − 1.
What is the answer?

○ ○ ○ ○ ○ ○

Answer _____

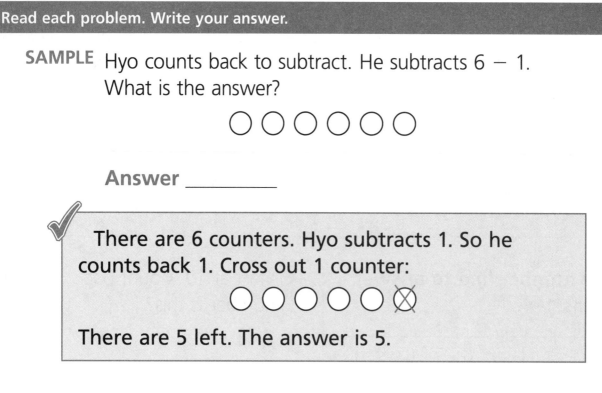

There are 6 counters. Hyo subtracts 1. So he counts back 1. Cross out 1 counter:

○ ○ ○ ○ ○ ⊗

There are 5 left. The answer is 5.

7 Ann has 4 pennies. She gets 3 more. Count on to add.

4   ____ ____ ____

8 Count back to subtract. Subtract 15 − 6.

○ ○ ○ ○ ○ ○ ○ ○ ○ ○ ○ ○ ○ ○ ○

Answer _____

9 Use the number line. Start at 9. Count on seven.
What numbers do you say?

```
◄──┼──┼──┼──┼──┼──┼──┼──┼──┼──┼──┼──┼──┼──┼──┼──┼──┼──┼──┼──┼──►
   0  1  2  3  4  5  6  7  8  9 10 11 12 13 14 15 16 17 18 19 20
```

Answer _____

UNIT 2 ▨▨▨▨▨▨▨▨▨▨▨▨▨▨▨▨▨▨▨▨▨▨▨▨
Understanding Addition and Subtraction

© The Continental Press, Inc.   DUPLICATING THIS MATERIAL IS ILLEGAL.

10 Jeff found 3 shells. Mei found 7 shells.

Jeff

Mei

Start with the greater number. Then count on.

Part A Find how many in all. Count on to add. What numbers do you say?

Answer _____

Part B Mei gave away 5 of her shells. Count back to subtract. Use the number line.

How many shells does Mei have left?

Answer _____

© The Continental Press, Inc.   DUPLICATING THIS MATERIAL IS ILLEGAL.

Addition and Subtraction Strategies

1.OA.6

Add to put groups together. **Subtract** to take a group apart.

Make 10. Then count on from 10.

Make 10 to help you add.

What is 8 + 4?

Use a ten frame. Show 8.

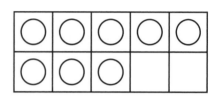

Add 4 counters. Fill in the ten frame.

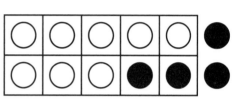

Look at the new addition sentence: $10 + 2 = \square$

Add: $10 + 2 = 12$. So $8 + 4 = 12$.

Addition facts help you with subtraction facts. Think of the addition fact. Use it to find the subtraction fact.

A **fact family** shows related facts. It has three numbers. One is a total. The other two are parts.

What facts are in this fact family?

Write addition sentences. Add the parts.

Part	Part
8	4
Total	
12	

$$8 + 4 = 12 \qquad 4 + 8 = 12$$

Write subtraction sentences. Subtract the parts from the total.

$$12 - 8 = 4 \qquad 12 - 4 = 8$$

UNIT 2 ▓▓▓▓▓▓▓▓▓▓▓▓▓▓▓▓▓▓▓▓▓▓▓▓▓▓▓▓▓▓▓▓▓
Understanding Addition and Subtraction

© The Continental Press, Inc.   DUPLICATING THIS MATERIAL IS ILLEGAL.

SAMPLE Dion adds 9 + 6. What make-10 fact could he use?

A 9 + 10   C 10 + 6

B 10 + 5   D 9 + 6 + 10

> ✔ The correct answer is B. Use a ten frame. There are 9 counters. There are 6 more counters. Put 1 more in the ten frame. There are 5 outside. The fact is 10 + 5.

1 Cassie subtracts 15 − 8. Which addition sentence can help her?

A 15 + 8 = 23

B 8 + 10 = 18

C 8 + 7 = 15

D 3 + 12 = 15

2 Steve added 6 + 8. He makes ten. Which shows what Steve did?

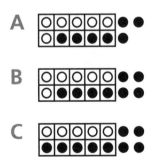

3 Look at this fact family.

4 + 7 = 11   11 − 4 = 7

7 + 4 = 11   ?

Which number sentence is missing?

A 11 − 7 = 4

B 11 − 9 = 2

C 11 + 7 = 18

D 11 + 4 = 15

4 What addition sentence does this ten frame show?

A 4 + 6 = 10

B 2 + 8 = 10

C 10 + 3 = 13

D 8 + 5 = 13

© The Continental Press, Inc.   DUPLICATING THIS MATERIAL IS ILLEGAL.

SAMPLE Look at this addition fact.

$$9 + 8 = 17$$

What is a related subtraction fact?

Answer _____

> ✓ Use the same three numbers. The numbers 9 and 8 are parts. The number 17 is the whole. Subtract one of the parts from the whole. The answer is the other part. You could write $17 - 9 = 8$. You could also write $17 - 8 = 9$. These are both related facts.

5 Write the addition sentence shown. Then write the make-10 fact.

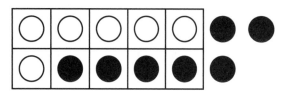

Addition sentence _____

Make-10 fact _____

6 Write the facts in this fact family.
There are two addition sentences.
There are two subtraction sentences.

Part	Part
9	5
Total	
14	

Addition sentences _____

Subtraction sentences _____

© The Continental Press, Inc.   DUPLICATING THIS MATERIAL IS ILLEGAL.

7 Lana adds 5 + 7.

Part A Use this ten frame to add 5 + 7.
Write the sum.

Answer _____

Part B Lana writes a related subtraction
fact. What are the two related
subtraction facts?

Look at the
three numbers in
part A. A related
fact has the
same numbers.

Answer _____

_____

© The Continental Press, Inc.   DUPLICATING THIS MATERIAL IS ILLEGAL.

More Addition and Subtraction Strategies

1.OA.6

You can break a number apart. Make a doubles plus 1 fact.

Add: 6 + 7

Think: 7 = 6 + 1

Add: 6 + 6 + 1 = 12 + 1 = 13

Use a doubles fact to subtract.

10 − 5 = ☐

Think: 5 + 5 = 10

10 − 5 = 5

Take a number apart to subtract. This is like "making ten."

Subtract: 12 − 4

Think: 12 is 2 more than 10

Think: 4 is 2 + 2

Subtract: 12 − 2 = 10, 10 − 2 = 8

12 − 4 = 8

Doubles facts help you add. A doubles fact shows a number added to itself.

What doubles fact is shown here?

Look at the first group. Count the muffins: 5

Look at the second group. Count the muffins: 5

Put the groups together: 5 + 5

There are 10 muffins in all. The doubles fact is 5 + 5 = 10.

What is 5 + 6?

Use a doubles fact plus 1. You know the doubles fact: 5 + 5 = 10

Find 1 more than 10: 11

There are 11 muffins. So 5 + 6 = 11.

Take a number apart. This can help you subtract.

Subtract 11 − 6.

Think of 6 as two numbers: 1 + 5

First subtract 1: 11 − 1 = 10

Then subtract 5: 10 − 5 = 5

So 11 − 6 = 5.

© The Continental Press, Inc.   DUPLICATING THIS MATERIAL IS ILLEGAL.

SAMPLE What doubles fact does this picture show?

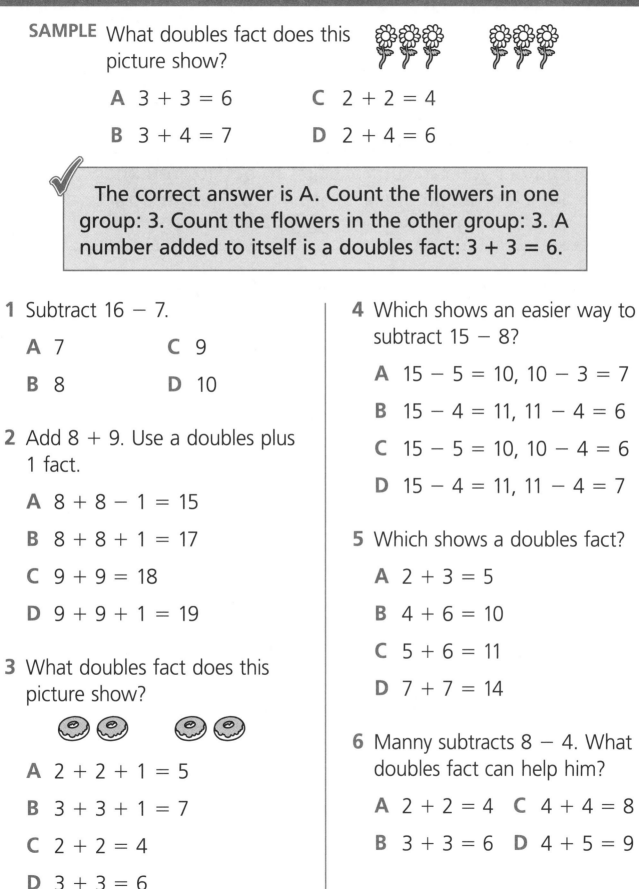

A 3 + 3 = 6   C 2 + 2 = 4

B 3 + 4 = 7   D 2 + 4 = 6

✓ The correct answer is A. Count the flowers in one group: 3. Count the flowers in the other group: 3. A number added to itself is a doubles fact: 3 + 3 = 6.

1 Subtract 16 − 7.

A 7   C 9

B 8   D 10

2 Add 8 + 9. Use a doubles plus 1 fact.

A 8 + 8 − 1 = 15

B 8 + 8 + 1 = 17

C 9 + 9 = 18

D 9 + 9 + 1 = 19

3 What doubles fact does this picture show?

A 2 + 2 + 1 = 5

B 3 + 3 + 1 = 7

C 2 + 2 = 4

D 3 + 3 = 6

4 Which shows an easier way to subtract 15 − 8?

A 15 − 5 = 10, 10 − 3 = 7

B 15 − 4 = 11, 11 − 4 = 6

C 15 − 5 = 10, 10 − 4 = 6

D 15 − 4 = 11, 11 − 4 = 7

5 Which shows a doubles fact?

A 2 + 3 = 5

B 4 + 6 = 10

C 5 + 6 = 11

D 7 + 7 = 14

6 Manny subtracts 8 − 4. What doubles fact can help him?

A 2 + 2 = 4   C 4 + 4 = 8

B 3 + 3 = 6   D 4 + 5 = 9

© The Continental Press, Inc.   DUPLICATING THIS MATERIAL IS ILLEGAL.

SAMPLE Subtract 14 − 9. Take 9 apart to make it easier.

Answer _____

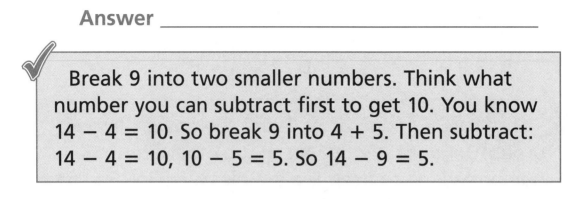

Break 9 into two smaller numbers. Think what number you can subtract first to get 10. You know 14 − 4 = 10. So break 9 into 4 + 5. Then subtract: 14 − 4 = 10, 10 − 5 = 5. So 14 − 9 = 5.

7 Look at this picture. Write the doubles fact. Find the sum.

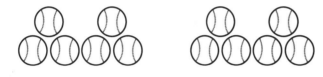

Answer _____

8 Subtract 13 − 6. Take 6 apart to make it easier. Show what you did.

Answer _____

9 How can knowing 7 + 7 help you find the sum for 7 + 8?

_____

_____

© The Continental Press, Inc. DUPLICATING THIS MATERIAL IS ILLEGAL.

10 Look at this picture.

Part A Write the doubles fact for this picture. Find the sum.

Answer _____

Part B Draw 1 more fish in the second group. What is the new addition fact? Tell how you can use the doubles fact to find the sum.

What kind of fact is this now?

_____

_____

_____

_____

© The Continental Press, Inc.   DUPLICATING THIS MATERIAL IS ILLEGAL.

Properties of Operations

1.OA.3

Rules can help you take shortcuts.

Use a shortcut in the first problem. You do not need to add. Look at what you know:

Jill has 2 + 3 beads.

Erica has 3 + 2 beads.

You can add numbers in any order

So 2 + 3 = 3 + 2.

They have the same number of beads.

Look for numbers that are easy to add first.

• Look for numbers that sum to 10.

• Look for doubles facts.

Some rules help you add.

You can add numbers in any order. The sum is the same.

Who has more beads, Jill or Erica?

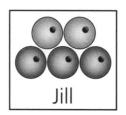
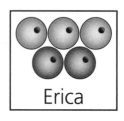

Jill   Erica

Add Jill's beads: 2 green beads + 3 black beads = 5 beads

Add Erica's beads: 3 green beads + 2 black beads = 5 beads

The girls have the same number of beads.

You can add three numbers. Group the numbers. You can group them in any order. The sum is the same.

Add 4 + 3 + 6.

$$\begin{array}{l} 4 \\ 3 \\ \underline{+6} \\ 13 \end{array}$$ Add: 4 + 3 = 7

Add: 7 + 6 = 13

$$\begin{array}{l} 4 \\ 3 \\ \underline{+6} \\ 13 \end{array}$$ Add: 4 + 6 = 10

Add: 10 + 3 = 13

The sum of 4 + 3 + 6 is 13.

© The Continental Press, Inc.   DUPLICATING THIS MATERIAL IS ILLEGAL.

SAMPLE Find the sum.

$$3 + 6 + 7 = \square$$

A 15   B 16   C 17   D 18

✓ The correct answer is B. You can add the numbers in any order. Pick two numbers: 3 + 7 = 10. Then add the last number: 10 + 6 = 16. The sum is 16.

1 Which is the same as 4 + 8?

    A 4 + 9

    B 3 + 7

    C 8 + 4

    D 8 + 5

2 Brad rolled three dice.

What is the sum of Brad's roll?

    A 8   C 10

    B 9   D 11

3 Find the sum.

$$9 + 3 + 1 = \square$$

    A 10   C 13

    B 12   D 14

4 Look at this picture.

Which two addition facts show this picture?

    A 2 + 6 = 8
        6 + 2 = 8

    B 2 + 6 = 8
        8 + 2 = 10

    C 6 + 2 = 8
        8 + 6 = 14

    D 6 + 2 = 8
        4 + 4 = 8

© The Continental Press, Inc.   DUPLICATING THIS MATERIAL IS ILLEGAL.

SAMPLE Amber has 3 blue ribbons. She has 6 red ribbons. Emi has 6 blue ribbons. She has 3 red ribbons. Who has more ribbons? Tell how you know.

Answer _____

✓ You do not need to add. Amber has 3 + 6 ribbons. Emi has 6 + 3 ribbons. You know you can add number in any order. The sum is the same. Both girls have the same number of ribbons.

5 Add.
Circle the numbers you added first.

$$
\begin{array}{r}
2 \\
4 \\
+2 \\
\hline
\end{array}
$$

Answer _____

6 Look at this picture.

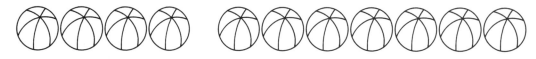

Write two addition facts for this picture.

Answer _____

7 Tell how you would find the sum of 8 + 3 + 7.

_____

_____

© The Continental Press, Inc.   DUPLICATING THIS MATERIAL IS ILLEGAL.

8 These numbers are in a hat.

| 5 | 4 | 1 | 5 | 2 | 1 |

Part A Luc pulled three numbers. The sum of his numbers was 12. Which numbers did Luc pull?

Look for numbers that are easy to add.

Answer _____

Part B Tell how you know you are correct.

_____

_____

_____

_____

© The Continental Press, Inc.   DUPLICATING THIS MATERIAL IS ILLEGAL.

REVIEW

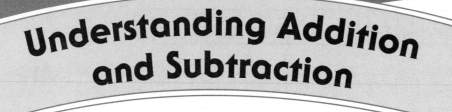

Understanding Addition and Subtraction

Read each problem. Circle the letter of the best answer.

1 Start at 4. Count on 2. What number is this?

A 2   C 5

B 4   D 6

2 Look at this fact family.

$5 + 6 = 11$ $11 - 6 = 5$

? $11 - 5 = 6$

What fact is missing?

A $5 + 5 = 10$

B $6 + 5 = 11$

C $7 + 4 = 11$

D $11 + 6 = 17$

3 Which shows a doubles fact?

A $6 + 6 = 12$

B $4 + 8 = 12$

C $7 + 8 = 15$

D $5 + 4 = 9$

4 What two addition facts does this picture show?

A $1 + 1 = 2, 4 + 4 = 8$

B $1 + 4 = 5, 5 + 1 = 6$

C $1 + 4 = 5, 4 + 1 = 5$

D $4 + 1 = 5, 2 + 3 = 5$

5 Add $8 + 3 + 2$.

A 10   C 12

B 11   D 13

6 Gabe starts at 15. He counts back 5. What numbers does he say?

A 15, 14, 13, 12

B 14, 13, 12, 11, 10

C 15, 14, 13, 12, 11

D 14, 13, 12, 11

© The Continental Press, Inc.   DUPLICATING THIS MATERIAL IS ILLEGAL.

7 Use this ten frame to add 4 + 7. Write the sum.

Answer _____

8 Look at this picture.

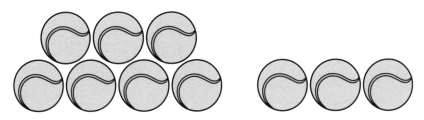

Write two addition facts for this picture.

Answer _____

9 Use the number line.

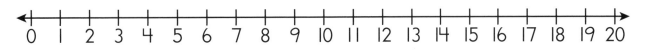

Subtract 17 − 8.

Answer _____

10 Subtract 14 − 6. Take 6 apart to make it easier.
Show what you did.

Answer _____

© The Continental Press, Inc.   DUPLICATING THIS MATERIAL IS ILLEGAL.

11 Look at the ten frame below.

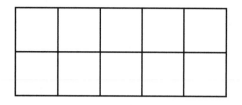

Part A Use the ten frame to add 8 + 9. What is the sum?

Answer _____

Part B What doubles plus 1 fact can help you add 8 + 9? Tell how you know.

_____

_____

_____

_____

© The Continental Press, Inc.   DUPLICATING THIS MATERIAL IS ILLEGAL.

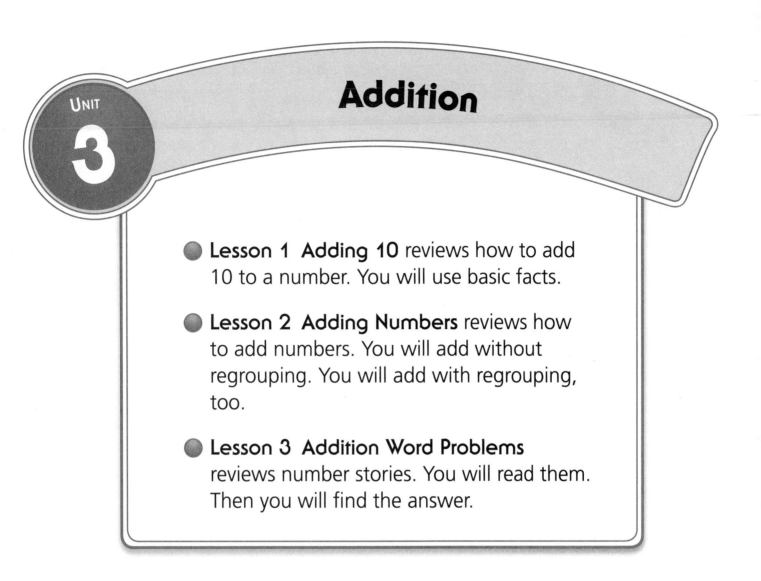

Addition

UNIT 3

- **Lesson 1 Adding 10** reviews how to add 10 to a number. You will use basic facts.

- **Lesson 2 Adding Numbers** reviews how to add numbers. You will add without regrouping. You will add with regrouping, too.

- **Lesson 3 Addition Word Problems** reviews number stories. You will read them. Then you will find the answer.

© The Continental Press, Inc.   DUPLICATING THIS MATERIAL IS ILLEGAL.

Adding 10

1.NBT.4, 1.NBT.5

> You can add 10 in your head. Add 1 to the tens. The ones stay the same.
>
> Tens are:
>
> | | |
> |---|---|
> | 10 | 60 |
> | 20 | 70 |
> | 30 | 80 |
> | 40 | 90 |
> | 50 | |

You can add 10 to a number without counting.

What is 35 + 10?

Think of 35 as 3 tens and 5 ones.

Think of 10 as 1 ten.

Add 1 to the tens:

3 tens + 1 ten = 4 tens

The ones stay the same.

So 35 + 10 = 45.

Tens	Ones

Use basic facts to add tens.

What is 30 + 20?

Think of 30 as 3 tens.

Think of 20 as 2 tens.

Think of the basic fact: 3 + 2 = 5

Add:

$$
\begin{array}{r} 3 \text{ tens} \\ +2 \text{ tens} \\ \hline 5 \text{ tens} \end{array}
\qquad
\begin{array}{r} 30 \\ +20 \\ \hline 50 \end{array}
$$

So 30 + 20 = 50.

© The Continental Press, Inc. DUPLICATING THIS MATERIAL IS ILLEGAL.

SAMPLE What is 10 more than 28?

A 18   **B** 20   **C** 30   **D** 38

> The correct answer is D. Add 10 to 28. Add 1 to the tens place: 2 + 1 = 3. The ones stay the same. So 10 more than 28 is 38.

1 Find the sum.

$$\begin{array}{r} 50 \\ +30 \\ \hline \end{array}$$

A 35   **C** 80

B 53   **D** 90

2 Add 10 to 67. What is the sum?

A 68

B 77

C 78

D 80

3 Add 10 + 40. What basic fact can you use?

A 1 + 4

B 2 + 2

C 2 + 3

D 1 + 5

4 What is 10 more than 41?

A 31

B 42

C 50

D 51

5 What is 20 + 20?

A 22

B 40

C 42

D 50

6 Add:

$$\begin{array}{r} 74 \\ +10 \\ \hline \end{array}$$

A 75

B 80

C 84

D 90

© The Continental Press, Inc.   DUPLICATING THIS MATERIAL IS ILLEGAL.

SAMPLE Add 60 + 20.

Answer _____

> Add the tens. Look at the numbers in the tens place. Use the basic fact 6 + 2 = 8. So 60 + 20 = 80.

7 What is 10 more than 54?

Answer _____

8 Ian wants to add 40 + 50. What basic fact can he use?

Answer _____

9 Suki adds 33 + 20. Tell how she can do this in her head.

_____

_____

_____

_____

© The Continental Press, Inc.   DUPLICATING THIS MATERIAL IS ILLEGAL.

10 Parker has these blocks. The blocks show two numbers.

Part A Write an addition sentence with the numbers. Find the sum.

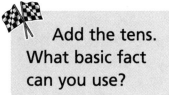

Add the tens. What basic fact can you use?

Answer _____

Part B Parker adds one more tens block. What is the sum now? Tell how you know.

_____

_____

_____

_____

© The Continental Press, Inc.   DUPLICATING THIS MATERIAL IS ILLEGAL.

Adding Numbers

1.NBT.4

Use tens and ones blocks to help you add.

$$\text{||||} = 10$$

$$\square = 1$$

Always add the ones first. Then add the tens. Be careful when you line up the numbers.

64 + 2 is

$$\begin{array}{r} 64 \\ +\ 2 \end{array} \quad \textbf{not} \quad \begin{array}{r} 64 \\ +2 \end{array}$$

Ten ones is the same as one ten.

Always regroup when there are 10 or more ones.

$$\square\square\square\square\square = \text{|||}$$

Add to put together.

Add: 23 + 15

Line up the digits.

Add the ones:
3 ones + 5 ones = 8 ones

Add the tens:
2 tens + 1 ten = 3 tens

The sum is 38.

$$23 \qquad 15$$

$$\begin{array}{r} 23 \\ +15 \\ \hline 8 \end{array} \qquad \begin{array}{r} 23 \\ +15 \\ \hline 38 \end{array}$$

Regroup when the sum of the ones is 10 or more.

Add: 28 + 15

Add the ones:
8 ones + 5 ones = 13 ones

Regroup 10 ones as 1 ten.

Write 3 in the ones place. Write 1 over the tens place.

$$28 \qquad 15$$

$$\begin{array}{r} \overset{1}{2}8 \\ +15 \\ \hline 3 \end{array}$$

Add the tens:
1 ten + 2 tens + 1 ten = 4 tens

Write 4 in the tens place.

$$\begin{array}{r} \overset{1}{2}8 \\ +15 \\ \hline 43 \end{array}$$

The sum is 43.

UNIT 3
Addition

© The Continental Press, Inc.   DUPLICATING THIS MATERIAL IS ILLEGAL.

SAMPLE Look at this chart. Find the sum.

A 73   C 83

B 74   D 84

Tens	Ones
5 +2	1 3

The correct answer is B. The chart shows the ones and the tens. First add the ones: 1 one + 3 ones = 4 ones. Then add the tens: 5 tens + 2 tens = 7 tens. The number with 7 tens and 4 ones is 74.

1 Add:

$$17 + 4 = \square$$

A 11   C 47

B 21   D 57

2 Find the sum.

$$\begin{array}{r} 62 \\ +29 \\ \hline \end{array}$$

A 81   C 91

B 90   D 99

3 Add:

$$\begin{array}{r} 42 \\ +33 \\ \hline \end{array}$$

A 75   C 85

B 76   D 86

4 Look at this chart.

Tens	Ones
3 +6	4 4

What is the sum?

A 87   C 97

B 88   D 98

5 Add:

$$38 + 12 = \square$$

A 30   C 50

B 40   D 60

© The Continental Press, Inc. DUPLICATING THIS MATERIAL IS ILLEGAL.

SAMPLE Add 53 + 39.

Answer _____

> Line up the numbers. Line up the ones. Line up the tens. Add the ones: 3 + 9 = 12 ones. Regroup. 12 ones is 1 ten and 2 ones. Add the tens: 1 + 5 + 3 = 9 tens. So 53 + 39 = 92.
>
> $$\begin{array}{r} 1 \\ 53 \\ +39 \\ \hline 92 \end{array}$$

6 Find the sum. Write your answer in the box. Show your work.

Tens	Ones
1 +7	8 7

7 Meg wants to add 31 + 28. Does she need to regroup? Tell how you know.

_____

_____

8 Add 27 + 5. Show your work.

Answer _____

© The Continental Press, Inc. DUPLICATING THIS MATERIAL IS ILLEGAL.

9 Look at the blocks. They show two numbers.

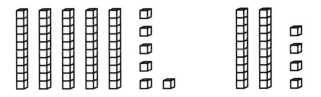

Part A Add these numbers. Write them in the chart.

Tens	Ones
+	

> Be careful when you line up the numbers. Line up the tens. Line up the ones.

Part B Hector moved 1 ones block. He took it from the second number. He put it with the first number. Now the blocks look like this.

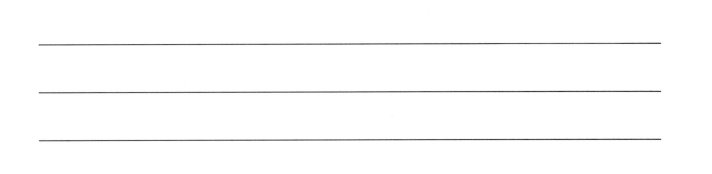

Look at the new numbers. Tell how you know the sum without adding.

_____

_____

_____

_____

© The Continental Press, Inc.   DUPLICATING THIS MATERIAL IS ILLEGAL.

Addition Word Problems

1.OA.1, 1.OA.2

How to solve number stories:

1. Read
2. Plan
3. Solve
4. Check

Use subtraction to check addition.

Check if $3 + 1 = 4$.

Subtract: $4 - 1 = 3$

The addition is correct.

There are different ways to find an answer to a number story. Use the one that works for you.

1. Write a number sentence.
2. Use number blocks.
3. Make a drawing.

You can add three numbers in any order. The sum is always the same.

You can add to solve **number stories.** Read the story first. Make a plan to find the answer. Then do the work. Always check your answer.

Ryan has 9 books. Malik has 5 books. How many do they have in all?

Make a plan. Add to find how many books.

Find the important facts:

Ryan's books: 9   Malik's books: 5

Do the work. Add: $9 + 5 = 14$

The boys have 14 books in all.

You can draw a picture to help you find the answer.

Becky picked 4 flowers. Angel picked 8 flowers. Molly picked 5 flowers. How many flowers did they pick in all?

Make a plan. Add to find how many in all.

Draw a picture:

Becky: 🌼🌼🌼🌼

Angel: 🌼🌼🌼🌼🌼🌼🌼🌼

Molly: 🌼🌼🌼🌼🌼

Do the work. Count the flowers: 17

So $4 + 8 + 5 = 17$. They picked 17 flowers.

© The Continental Press, Inc.   DUPLICATING THIS MATERIAL IS ILLEGAL.

SAMPLE A bag holds 2 green marbles. It has 6 red marbles. It has 4 blue marbles. How many marbles are there in all?

A 8   B 10   C 12   D 14

The correct answer is C. Find the number of marbles. Add the three numbers. Write: 2 + 6 + 4 = □. You can add three numbers in any order. Add: 6 + 4 = 10, 10 + 2 = 12. There are 12 marbles in all.

1 A toy train has 12 cars. Then 2 more cars are added. How many cars are there in all?

A 10   C 15

B 14   D 24

2 A tray has 3 chocolate cookies. It has 9 sugar cookies. It has 3 peanut butter cookies. How many cookies are there in all?

A 6   C 14

B 12   D 15

3 Sarah colored 7 pictures. Then she colored 7 more pictures. How many did she color in all?

A 7   C 13

B 10   D 14

4 Austin listened to 8 songs. Keiko listened to 3 songs. Owen listened to 5 songs. Find how many songs in all. Which number sentence can you use?

A 8 + 3 + 5 = □

B 8 + 3 − 5 = □

C 8 + 3 = □

D 3 + 5 = □

5 Tony did 10 sit-ups. Rob did 9 sit-ups. How many sit-ups did they do in all?

A 1

B 18

C 19

D 20

© The Continental Press, Inc. DUPLICATING THIS MATERIAL IS ILLEGAL.

SAMPLE There are 3 bananas in a basket. There are 11 bananas in a box. How many bananas are there in all?

Answer _____

> ✓ Add the numbers. Draw a picture to help. Draw 3 bananas. Then draw 11 bananas.
>
> There are 14 bananas in all.

6 Justin has 5 pennies. He gets 13 more pennies. How many pennies does he have in all? Show your work.

Answer _____

7 Each box holds some jump ropes.

How many jump ropes are there in all?

Answer _____

7 Jump Ropes

4 Jump Ropes   6 Jump Ropes

8 Laura ate 4 grapes. Chula ate 16 grapes. How many grapes did they eat in all? Show your work.

Answer _____

UNIT 3 ▓▓▓▓▓▓▓▓▓▓▓▓▓▓▓▓▓▓▓▓▓▓▓▓▓▓▓▓▓▓▓▓
Addition

© The Continental Press, Inc.   DUPLICATING THIS MATERIAL IS ILLEGAL.

9 There were 8 ducks at a pond. Then 5 more ducks came.

Part A How many ducks were there in all? Draw a picture.

Read carefully. Make a plan. Then do the work.

Answer _____

Part B Check your answer. Use subtraction. Tell why you can do this.

_____

_____

_____

_____

© The Continental Press, Inc.   DUPLICATING THIS MATERIAL IS ILLEGAL.

REVIEW

Addition

Read each problem. Circle the letter of the best answer.

1 Add 20 + 40. What basic fact can you use?

  A 1 + 5 = 6

  B 2 + 4 = 6

  C 4 + 4 = 8

  D 2 + 2 = 4

2 A necklace has 9 beads. Lily puts 6 more beads on. How many beads are there now?

  A 13

  B 14

  C 15

  D 16

3 Add 17 + 59.

  A 76   **C** 66

  B 75   **D** 65

4 There were 7 cats. There were 4 dogs. There were 5 mice. How many animals were there in all?

  A 9   **C** 16

  B 11   **D** 17

5 Find the sum.

$$\begin{array}{r} 36 \\ +21 \\ \hline \end{array}$$

  A 56   **C** 66

  B 57   **D** 67

6 What is 10 more than 59?

  A 50

  B 60

  C 68

  D 69

UNIT 3
Addition

© The Continental Press, Inc.   DUPLICATING THIS MATERIAL IS ILLEGAL.

7 Zoe has 11 cards in a game. She pulls 4 more. How many cards does she have now? Show your work.

Answer _____

8 Add 43 + 48. Use this chart.

Tens	Ones
+	

9 Tell how to find 10 more than 31.

_____

_____

10 There were 6 orange hats. There were 2 blue hats. There were 11 green hats. How many hats were there in all? Show your work.

Answer _____

© The Continental Press, Inc. DUPLICATING THIS MATERIAL IS ILLEGAL.

11 Look at these numbers.

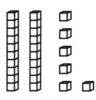

Part A Add these numbers. Show your work.

Answer _____

Part B Heidi changed the second number. She added some tens blocks. Now the number looks like this:

What is the sum of the two numbers now? Tell how you know.

_____

_____

_____

_____

UNIT 3 ▨▨▨▨▨▨▨▨▨▨▨▨▨▨▨▨▨▨▨▨▨▨▨▨▨▨▨
Addition

© The Continental Press, Inc.   DUPLICATING THIS MATERIAL IS ILLEGAL.

Subtraction

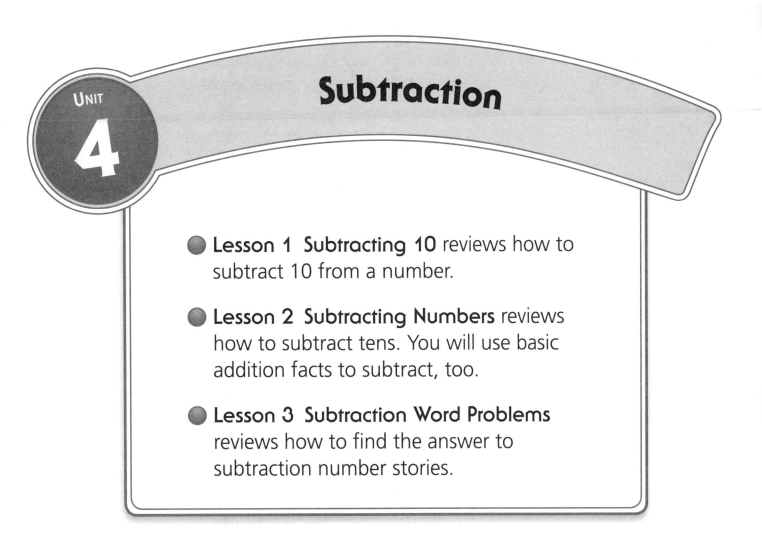

● **Lesson 1 Subtracting 10** reviews how to subtract 10 from a number.

● **Lesson 2 Subtracting Numbers** reviews how to subtract tens. You will use basic addition facts to subtract, too.

● **Lesson 3 Subtraction Word Problems** reviews how to find the answer to subtraction number stories.

© The Continental Press, Inc.   DUPLICATING THIS MATERIAL IS ILLEGAL.

Subtracting 10

1.NBT.5

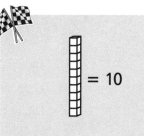

= 10

Subtract 10 in your head. Take 1 away from the tens place. Do not change the ones.

You can subtract 10 without counting. You can do it in your head.

What is 24 − 10?

Think of 24 as 2 tens and 4 ones.

Think of 10 as 1 ten.

Subtract the tens: 2 tens − 1 ten = 1 ten

The ones stay the same.

So, 24 − 10 = 14.

This model shows 24. Take away 1 ten.

Tens	Ones

So 24 − 10 = 14.

© The Continental Press, Inc.   DUPLICATING THIS MATERIAL IS ILLEGAL.

SAMPLE What is 10 less than 99?

A 100   **B** 90   **C** 89   **D** 79

> The correct answer is C. Subtract 99 − 10. Subtract 1 from the tens place: 9 − 1 = 8. The ones stay the same. So 10 less than 99 is 89.

1 Subtract:
$$\begin{array}{r} 16 \\ -10 \\ \hline \end{array}$$

A 26

B 16

C 10

D 6

2 What is 10 less than 52?

A 50

B 42

C 40

D 32

3 Find 10 less than 67.

A 57

B 66

C 70

D 77

4 Subtract.

$$84 - 10 = \square$$

A 83

B 80

C 74

D 73

5 What is 10 less than 10?

A 0

B 1

C 10

D 20

© The Continental Press, Inc. DUPLICATING THIS MATERIAL IS ILLEGAL.

SAMPLE Subtract 10 from 75.

Answer _____

✓ Think of 75 as 7 tens and 5 ones. Think of 10 as 1 ten. Subtract 1 ten. Now there are 6 tens and 5 ones. So the answer is 65.

6 Zack says 10 less than 43 is 33. Lance says it is 42. Who is right? Tell how you know.

_____

_____

_____

7 Find 10 less than 86.

Answer _____

8 Subtract.

$$19 - 10 = \square$$

Answer _____

© The Continental Press, Inc. DUPLICATING THIS MATERIAL IS ILLEGAL.

9 Look at this number sentence.

$$55 - 10 = \square$$

Part A What is the difference?

Answer _____

Part B Beth uses number blocks to show 55. She wants to find 10 less than 55. How can she change the number blocks to do this? Tell how you know.

> How many tens blocks does Beth have? How many does she take away?

_____

_____

_____

_____

© The Continental Press, Inc. DUPLICATING THIS MATERIAL IS ILLEGAL.

Subtracting Numbers

1.NBT.6, 1.OA.4

Tens are:

10	60
20	70
30	80
40	90
50	

Addition is the opposite of subtraction. Add to put together. Subtract to take apart.

Add to check subtraction. Add the answer and the number that was subtracted. The sum should be the first number.

Check: 5 − 2 = 3

Add: 3 + 2 = 5

You can use basic facts to help you subtract tens.

Subtract 70 − 20.

Think of 70 as 7 tens.

Think of 20 as 2 tens.

Think of the basic fact 7 − 2 = 5.

Subtract:

$$\begin{array}{r} 7 \text{ tens} \\ -2 \text{ tens} \\ \hline 5 \text{ tens} \end{array} \qquad \begin{array}{r} 70 \\ -20 \\ \hline 50 \end{array}$$

So 70 − 20 = 50.

Use addition to help you subtract. Write an addition sentence. Use a box for the number you do not know.

What is 10 − 8?

Think, "What number plus 8 is 10?"

Write: ☐ + 8 = 10

You know that 2 + 8 = 10. The missing number is 2.

So 10 − 8 = 2.

© The Continental Press, Inc.   DUPLICATING THIS MATERIAL IS ILLEGAL.

SAMPLE Subtract 15 − 7.

    A 6   **B** 7   **C** 8   **D** 9

> The correct answer is C. Think, "What number plus 7 is 15?" Use the basic addition fact: 8 + 7 = 15. So 15 − 7 = 8.

1 What is 50 − 20?

    A 20

    B 30

    C 40

    D 70

2 Dan wants to subtract 18 − 5. What addition sentence can Dan use?

    A 18 + □ = 5

    B 18 + 5 = □

    C 5 + 18 = □

    D 5 + □ = 18

3
$$\begin{array}{r} 80 \\ -40 \\ \hline \end{array}$$

    A 20   **C** 40

    B 30   **D** 50

4 What is 12 − 6?

    A 5   **C** 7

    B 6   **D** 8

5 Subtract:
$$\begin{array}{r} 14 \\ -5 \\ \hline \end{array}$$

    A 5

    B 6

    C 8

    D 9

6 Subtract 60 − 20. What basic fact can you use?

    A 6 − 2

    B 6 − 4

    C 6 + 2

    D 4 − 2

© The Continental Press, Inc. DUPLICATING THIS MATERIAL IS ILLEGAL.

SAMPLE Subtract 90 − 30. What basic fact can you use?

Answer _____

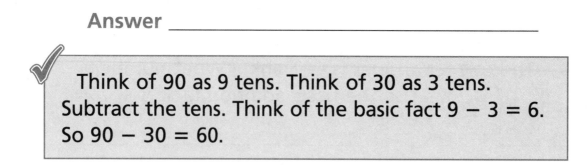

Think of 90 as 9 tens. Think of 30 as 3 tens.
Subtract the tens. Think of the basic fact 9 − 3 = 6.
So 90 − 30 = 60.

7 Yuri wants to subtract 18 − 10. Write an addition
sentence to help Yuri.

Answer _____

8 Subtract.

$$70 - 60 = \square$$

Answer _____

9

$$\begin{array}{r} 16 \\ -\ 9 \\ \hline \end{array}$$

Answer _____

© The Continental Press, Inc. DUPLICATING THIS MATERIAL IS ILLEGAL.

10 Val has these number blocks.

Part A Val takes away 3 blocks. Write a subtraction sentence to show this. Find the answer.

 What basic fact can you use?

Answer _____

Part B Val takes 2 more blocks away. Write a subtraction sentence. Find the answer. Tell how you know you are correct.

_____

_____

_____

_____

© The Continental Press, Inc. DUPLICATING THIS MATERIAL IS ILLEGAL.

Subtraction Word Problems

1.OA.1

How to solve number stories:

1. Read
2. Plan
3. Solve
4. Check

You can use different ways to solve a number story. Find one that works for you.

1. Write a number sentence.
2. Draw a picture.
3. Use number blocks.

Use addition to check subtraction.

Subtract to:

- Find how many more
- Find how many are left

You can subtract to solve number stories. Read the story first. Make a plan to find the answer. Then do the work. Always check your answer.

There were 13 birds. 4 birds flew away. How many are left?

Make a plan. Subtract to find how many are left.

Find the important facts.

> There were 13 birds at first.
> Then 4 birds flew away.

Do the work. Subtract: $13 - 4 = 9$

There are 9 birds left.

Check your answer. Add.

> 9 left + 4 that flew away = 13 in all

Niko has 12 pictures. Tisha has 8 pictures. How many more does Niko have than Tisha?

Make a plan. Subtract to find how many more.

Find the important facts.

> Niko's pictures: 12   Tisha's pictures: 8

Do the work. Subtract: $12 - 8 = 4$

Niko has 4 more pictures than Tisha.

© The Continental Press, Inc.   DUPLICATING THIS MATERIAL IS ILLEGAL.

SAMPLE There are 7 boys in line. Then 4 boys leave. How many boys are left?

A 2   B 3   C 4   D 11

The correct answer is B. Subtract to find how many are left. You can draw a picture.

So 7 − 4 = 3. There are 3 boys left.

1 There were 14 dolls on a shelf. People bought 7 of the dolls. How many dolls are left?

A 5

B 6

C 7

D 8

2 There are 10 green balls. There are 6 red balls. How many more green balls are there?

A 4

B 5

C 6

D 7

3 There were 16 girls at a party. Then 5 girls go home. How many girls are left?

A 5

B 7

C 9

D 11

4 There were 9 fish. Then 3 fish swam away. How many fish are left?

A 3

B 5

C 6

D 7

UNIT 4
Subtraction

© The Continental Press, Inc.   DUPLICATING THIS MATERIAL IS ILLEGAL.

SAMPLE There are 17 girls. There are 9 boys. How many more girls than boys are there?

Answer _____

Subtract to find how many more. Subtract: 17 − 9 = 8. There are 8 more girls.

5 There were 12 cars. Then 6 cars drove away. How many cars are left? Show your work.

Answer _____

6 Nala had these apples.

She ate 3 apples. How many apples are left?

Answer _____

7 There are 15 pens. There are 6 pencils. How many more pens than pencils are there? Show your work.

Answer _____

© The Continental Press, Inc.   DUPLICATING THIS MATERIAL IS ILLEGAL.

8 Scott has these coins.

Part A Scott gives 3 coins to his sister. How many does he have left? Show your work.

How can you use the picture to help you?

Answer _____

Part B Then Scott uses 10 coins. Now how many does he have left? Tell how you know.

_____

_____

_____

_____

© The Continental Press, Inc.   DUPLICATING THIS MATERIAL IS ILLEGAL.

REVIEW

Subtraction

Read each problem. Circle the letter of the best answer.

1 What is 10 less than 72?

A 52

B 60

C 62

D 70

2   18
         − 9

A 9

B 8

C 7

D 6

3 There were 13 cats. Then 6 cats walked away. How many cats were left?

A 6   C 8

B 7   D 9

4 Subtract: 40
                   −20

A 10   C 30

B 20   D 60

5 Ben wants to subtract 16 − 4. What addition sentence can he use?

A 16 + 4 = ☐

B 16 + ☐ = 4

C 4 + ☐ = 16

D 4 + 16 = ☐

6 Subtract 80 − 60. What basic fact can you use?

A 8 + 6

B 6 + 2

C 6 − 2

D 8 − 6

© The Continental Press, Inc.   DUPLICATING THIS MATERIAL IS ILLEGAL.

7 There were 14 flowers. Lin picked 7 flowers. How many flowers are left? Show your work.

Answer _____

8 How can you find 43 − 10 in your head? Tell what you did.

_____

_____

9 Subtract 70 − 50. Write the basic fact that helped you.

Answer _____

Basic fact _____

10 Subtract 15 − 9. Tell how you can use an addition fact to help you.

_____

_____

© The Continental Press, Inc.   DUPLICATING THIS MATERIAL IS ILLEGAL.

11 Hugo counted 17 stars. Erin counted 14 stars.

Part A How many more stars did Hugo count than Erin? Show your work.

Answer _____

Part B Tell how you found your answer.

_____

_____

_____

12 Look at the number model.

Part A Subtract 60 − 30. How can you use the model to help?

_____

_____

Part B What basic fact can help you subtract 60 − 30? Tell why it helps.

_____

_____

© The Continental Press, Inc.   DUPLICATING THIS MATERIAL IS ILLEGAL.

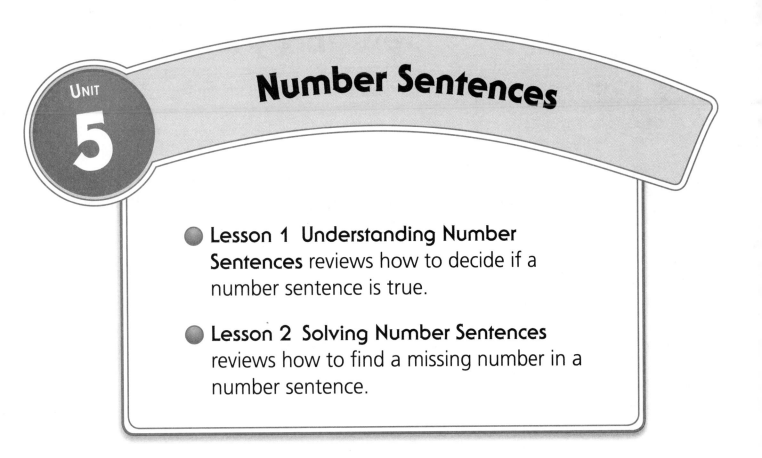

Number Sentences

UNIT 5

- **Lesson 1 Understanding Number Sentences** reviews how to decide if a number sentence is true.

- **Lesson 2 Solving Number Sentences** reviews how to find a missing number in a number sentence.

© The Continental Press, Inc.   DUPLICATING THIS MATERIAL IS ILLEGAL.

Understanding Number Sentences

LESSON 1

1.OA.7

The **plus sign** shows addition.

The **minus sign** shows subtraction.

A number sentence has numbers on both sides of the equal sign.

6 + 1 = 7
Number sentence

6 + 1
Not a number sentence

A **number sentence** shows numbers and signs. It can use the plus sign (+). It can use the minus sign (−). It can use the equal sign (=).

$$6 + 1 = 7 \quad 4 = 4 \quad 8 - 2 = 6 \quad 4 + 4 = 9 - 1$$

These are all number sentences.

The **equal sign** (=) means "is equal to." Equal means "the same."

$$6 + 1 = 7$$

This says, "6 plus 1 is the same as 7."

You can tell if a number sentence is true. Do the work.

Is this number sentence true?

$$6 + 1 = 9 - 2$$

The = splits the sentence into two parts.

First look at the left side: 6 + 1
Add: 6 + 1 = 7

Look at right side: 9 − 2
Subtract: 9 − 2 = 7

Ask, "Is 7 equal to 7?" Yes.

So 6 + 1 = 9 − 2 is true.

© The Continental Press, Inc.   DUPLICATING THIS MATERIAL IS ILLEGAL.

SAMPLE Which number sentence is true?

A $2 + 3 = 5 - 1$ C $2 + 2 = 5$

B $1 + 5 = 3 + 3$ D $4 - 1 = 2$

✓ The correct answer is B. Find the sum on each side of the equal sign: $1 + 5 = 6$ and $3 + 3 = 6$. Both sides equal 6. So the number sentence is true.

1 Look at part of a number sentence.

$$6 + 3 = \rule{2cm}{0.4pt}$$

Finish the number sentence. Which makes it true?

A $10 - 2$

B $4 + 4$

C $9 - 0$

D $5 + 6$

2 Which number sentence is **not** true?

A $4 + 6 = 6 + 4$

B $7 - 2 = 1 + 4$

C $8 - 6 = 1 + 1$

D $9 - 4 = 7 - 3$

3 Which number sentence is true?

A $12 - 4 = 8$

B $14 - 7 = 6$

C $12 - 5 = 6$

D $14 - 8 = 5$

4 Look at part of a number sentence.

$$\rule{2cm}{0.4pt} = 18 - 4$$

Finish the number sentence. Which makes it true?

A 4

B 12

C 14

D 15

© The Continental Press, Inc. DUPLICATING THIS MATERIAL IS ILLEGAL.

SAMPLE Frank wrote this number sentence.

$$5 + 2 = 4 + 4$$

Is this true? Tell how you know.

> Do the work. Add the numbers on the left: 5 + 2 = 7. Add the numbers on the right: 4 + 4 = 8. The number sentence says, "7 is the same as 8." This is not true.

5 Write a number sentence that is true. Use addition on the left. Use subtraction on the right.

Answer _____

6 Look at part of a number sentence.

$$10 - 5 = \underline{\hspace{1cm}}$$

Macy finished the number sentence. She used one number. What number did she use?

Answer _____

7 Look at this number sentence.

$$9 + 7 = 6 + 10$$

Is this true? Tell how you know.

_____

_____

_____

UNIT 5 ▨▨▨▨▨▨▨▨▨▨▨▨▨▨▨▨▨▨▨▨▨▨▨▨▨▨▨▨
Number Sentences

© The Continental Press, Inc.   DUPLICATING THIS MATERIAL IS ILLEGAL.

8 Tang wrote a number sentence. Grace wrote one, too.

Tang: $15 + 2 = 17 - 1$
Grace: $14 - 2 = 11 + 1$

Part A Whose number sentence is true? Tell how you know.

Do the work.
Add and subtract.

_____

_____

_____

_____

Part B Change the number sentence that is not true. Make it true. Change one number only.

Answer _____

© The Continental Press, Inc. DUPLICATING THIS MATERIAL IS ILLEGAL.

The missing number makes the number sentence true.

A ☐ stands for the missing number.

Look at the addition sentence. You can use subtraction.

$$7 + \square = 10$$
Subtract: $10 - 7 = 3$
$$\square = 3$$
Check: $7 + 3 = 10$

Check your work. Use the number you found.

Add to put together. Subtract to take apart.

Use **fact families** to find a missing number. They show related facts.

$$3 + 2 = \square$$
$$2 + 3 = \square$$
$$\square - 2 = 3$$
$$\square - 3 = 2$$

A number sentence shows numbers and signs. Sometimes a number is missing. You can find the missing number. Then you have **solved** the number sentence.

What is the missing number?

$$7 + \square = 10$$

This is an addition number sentence. It says, "7 plus a number equals 10."

You can count up to add. Start at 7. Count up until you get to 10: 8, 9, 10

You counted up 3.

The missing number is 3: $7 + 3 = 10$

What is the missing number?

$$\square - 2 = 3$$

This is a subtraction number sentence. It says, "A number minus 2 equals 3."

You can add. Add the two numbers. The sum is the missing number: $3 + 2 = 5$

The missing number is 5: $5 - 2 = 3$

© The Continental Press, Inc.   DUPLICATING THIS MATERIAL IS ILLEGAL.

SAMPLE Find the missing number.

$$8 - \square = 2$$

A 4   **B** 6   **C** 8   **D** 10

> The correct answer is B. This is a subtraction number sentence. It says, "8 minus a number is 2." Think of the fact family for 8, $\square$, and 2: $2 + \square = 8$, $\square + 2 = 8$, $8 - \square = 2$, and $8 - 2 = \square$. Use a related fact: $8 - 2 = \square$. Subtract to find the missing number: $8 - 2 = 6$. Check your work: $8 - 6 = 2$. The missing number is 6.

1 What is the missing number?

$$\square + 9 = 16$$

A 5   **C** 7

B 6   **D** 8

2 What number goes in the box?

$$\square - 4 = 10$$

A 6   **C** 12

B 8   **D** 14

3 Find the missing number.

$$15 - \square = 4$$

A 19   **C** 11

B 18   **D** 10

4 Look at the number sentence.

$$8 + \square = 16$$

What number is missing?

A 8   **C** 10

B 9   **D** 12

5 What is the missing number?

$$6 = 12 - \square$$

A 5   **C** 18

B 6   **D** 19

© The Continental Press, Inc.   DUPLICATING THIS MATERIAL IS ILLEGAL.

SAMPLE What is the missing number?

$$17 = 12 + \square$$

Answer _____

> ✓ Look at the number sentence. It is an addition sentence. Use subtraction. Subtract: $17 - 12 = 5$. You can also count up. Start at 12. Count up to 17: 13, 14, 15, 16, 17. You count up 5. The missing number is 5.

6 What number should go in the box?

$$\square - 3 = 12$$

Answer _____

7 Tell how to find the missing number.

$$8 + \square = 14$$

_____

_____

8 Subtract to find the missing number.

$$20 = \square + 4$$

Show your work.

Answer _____

© The Continental Press, Inc. DUPLICATING THIS MATERIAL IS ILLEGAL.

9 Look at this number sentence.

$$\square + 6 = 14$$

There are four facts in a fact family. They use the same three numbers.

Part A Write the fact family. Use the $\square$ for the missing number. Write the addition sentences. Write the subtraction sentences.

Addition sentences _____

Subtraction sentences _____

Part B Use one of these related facts. Find the missing number. Tell what you did.

_____

_____

_____

_____

© The Continental Press, Inc. DUPLICATING THIS MATERIAL IS ILLEGAL.

REVIEW

Number Sentences

Read each problem. Circle the letter of the best answer.

1 Which number sentence is true?

A $7 - 3 = 2 + 2$

B $4 + 1 = 3 + 3$

C $8 - 1 = 2 + 6$

D $5 - 2 = 3 + 4$

2 What is the missing number?

$$\square + 3 = 12$$

A 7   C 9

B 8   D 10

3 Look at part of a number sentence.

$$\underline{\quad\quad} = 16 - 2$$

Finish the number sentence. Which makes it true?

A $7 + 8$ C $8 + 8$

B $7 + 7$ D $8 + 9$

4 Find the missing number.

$$17 - \square = 7$$

A 8

B 9

C 10

D 11

5 Which number sentence is **not** true?

A $5 + 3 = 4 + 4$

B $2 + 7 = 10 - 1$

C $6 - 5 = 1 - 0$

D $9 - 4 = 2 + 2$

6 What number is missing?

$$11 = \square + 4$$

A 6   C 8

B 7   D 9

UNIT 5
Number Sentences

© The Continental Press, Inc.   DUPLICATING THIS MATERIAL IS ILLEGAL.

7 Write a number sentence that is true. Use subtraction on the left. Use addition on the right.

Answer _____

8 What number goes in the box?

$$\square - 6 = 12$$

Answer _____

9 Look at this number sentence.

$$9 + 8 = 7 + 11$$

Is this true? Tell how you know.

_____

_____

10 Tell how to find the missing number.

$$2 + \square = 13$$

_____

_____

© The Continental Press, Inc.   DUPLICATING THIS MATERIAL IS ILLEGAL.

11 Look at the number sentence below.

$$19 - 7 = 4 + 9$$

Part A Is this number sentence true? Tell how you know.

_____

_____

_____

_____

Part B Look at the left side. Change one number. Make the number sentence true. Write the new number sentence.

Answer _____

© The Continental Press, Inc.   DUPLICATING THIS MATERIAL IS ILLEGAL.

Measurement

UNIT 6

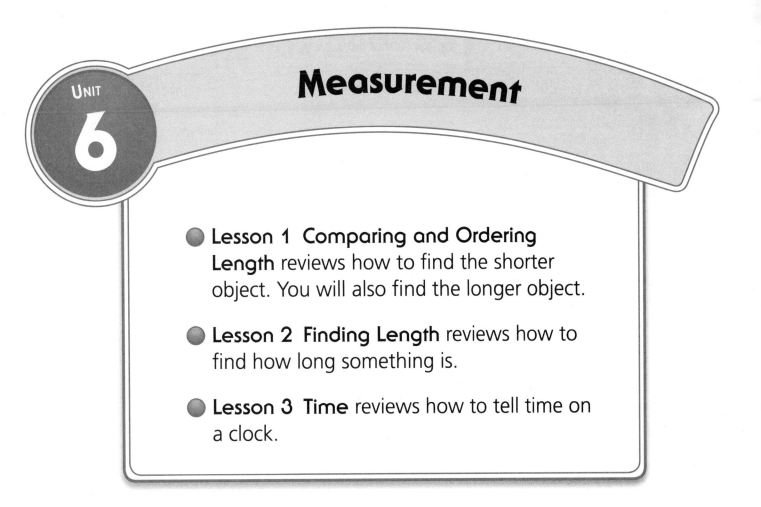

● **Lesson 1 Comparing and Ordering Length** reviews how to find the shorter object. You will also find the longer object.

● **Lesson 2 Finding Length** reviews how to find how long something is.

● **Lesson 3 Time** reviews how to tell time on a clock.

© The Continental Press, Inc.   DUPLICATING THIS MATERIAL IS ILLEGAL.

Comparing and Ordering Length

1.MD.1

Length is how long something is.

Use length to find how tall something is. Use it to find how wide something is.

You can put objects in another order. Start with the shortest object. End with the longest object.

Look at the ribbons. Start with the shortest ribbon. End with the longest ribbon.

A, C, B

You can compare lengths.

Which piece of string is longer?

A ▨▨▨▨▨▨▨▨

B ▨▨▨▨▨▨▨▨▨▨

Look at the pieces of string. Both pieces start at the same place. String A ends before string B.

String B is longer than string A. String A is shorter than string B.

Put objects in order. Use their lengths.

Put these ribbons in order. Start with the longest one. End with the shortest one.

A ▬▬▬▬

B ▬▬▬▬▬▬

C ▬▬▬▬

Find the longest ribbon. B is longer than A. B is longer than C. B is the longest.

Find the middle ribbon. C is longer than A. C is shorter than B. C is in the middle.

Find the shortest ribbon. A is shorter than B. A is shorter than C. A is the shortest.

Put them in order. Start with the longest: B, C, A

© The Continental Press, Inc.   DUPLICATING THIS MATERIAL IS ILLEGAL.

SAMPLE Look at this stick.

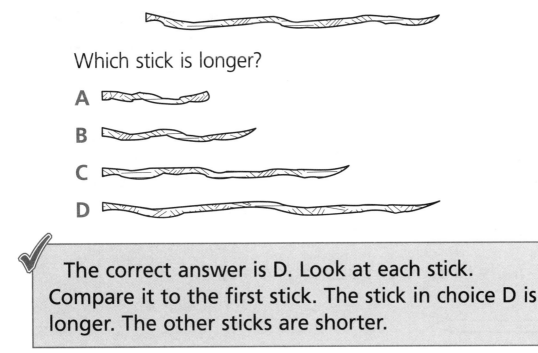

Which stick is longer?

A

B

C

D

✓ The correct answer is D. Look at each stick. Compare it to the first stick. The stick in choice D is longer. The other sticks are shorter.

1 Chase has these chains.

A

B

C

Chase puts the chains in order. He starts with the shortest chain. Which order is correct?

A A, B, C   **C** C, B, A

B C, A, B   **D** B, A, C

2 Rachel drew two lines. They have the same length. Which two lines did Rachel draw?

A   C

B   D

3 Dante has three blocks. They have different lengths. He put the blocks in a stack. The shortest block is on the top. The longest block is on the bottom. Which shows Dante's stack?

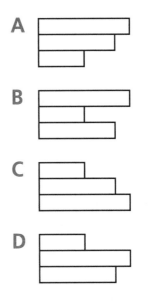

A

B

C

D

© The Continental Press, Inc.   DUPLICATING THIS MATERIAL IS ILLEGAL.

SAMPLE Put these lines in order. Start with the longest line. End with the shortest line.

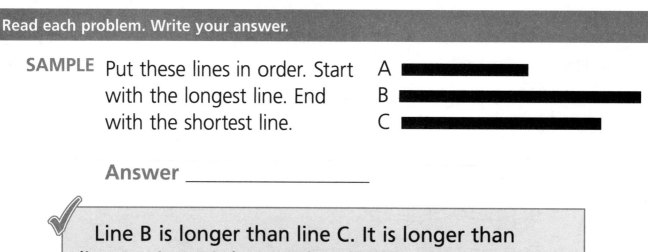

Answer _____

✓ Line B is longer than line C. It is longer than line A. Line C is longer than line A. Line A is the shortest. The order of the lines is B, C, A.

Use these nails to answer questions 4 and 5.

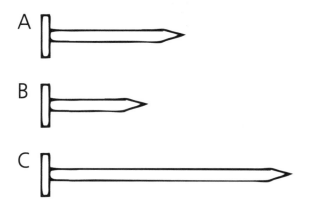

4 Mrs. Green has the nail shown below.

Which nail above is shorter than Mrs. Green's nail?

Answer _____

5 Put the nails in order. Start with the shortest nail. End with the longest nail.

Answer _____

© The Continental Press, Inc.   DUPLICATING THIS MATERIAL IS ILLEGAL.

6 Dawn has a pencil, a crayon, and a pen.

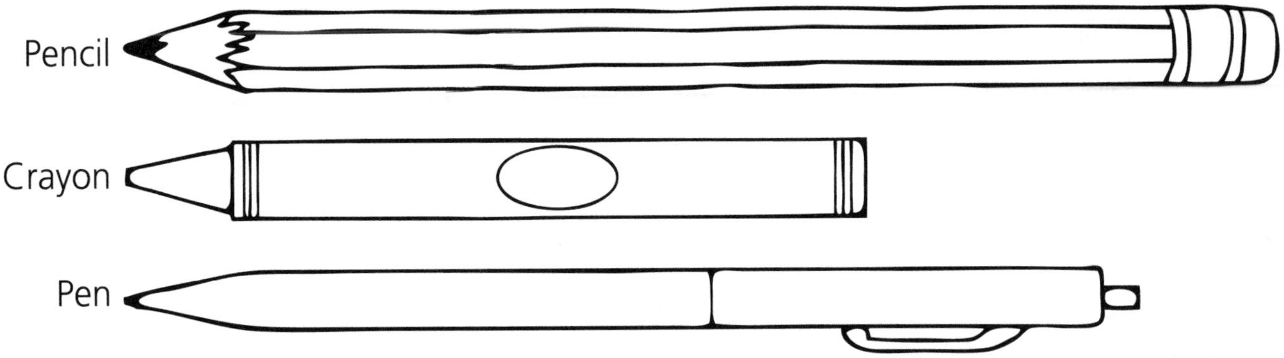

Pencil

Crayon

Pen

Part A Put the objects in order. Start with the longest object. End with the shortest object.

Look at the pencil. Is the crayon longer than the pencil? Is the pen longer than the pencil?

Answer _____

_____

Part B Dawn has another pencil. It is shown below.

Is this pencil longer than the first pencil? Tell how you know.

_____

_____

_____

_____

© The Continental Press, Inc.   DUPLICATING THIS MATERIAL IS ILLEGAL.

Finding Length

1.MD.2

You **measure** length. This means you use a tool to find how long something is.

Some other objects you can use to measure length are:

Pencil
Coin
Shoe

You can measure longer lengths with footsteps.

It is easier to measure a longer length with a longer object.

Hans measured the same toothbrush as Emma. The cubes are shorter than the paper clips. So it takes more cubes to measure the toothbrush. It takes less paper clips to measure the toothbrush.

You can use different objects to measure length.

Emma measured this toothbrush. How many paper clips did she use?

Count the paper clips under the toothbrush: 4

The toothbrush is 4 paper clips long.

Hans measured the toothbrush. He used cubes. How many cubes long is the toothbrush?

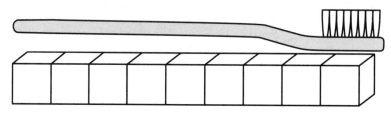

Hans could fit about 9 cubes under the toothbrush.

The toothbrush is about 9 cubes long.

© The Continental Press, Inc.   DUPLICATING THIS MATERIAL IS ILLEGAL.

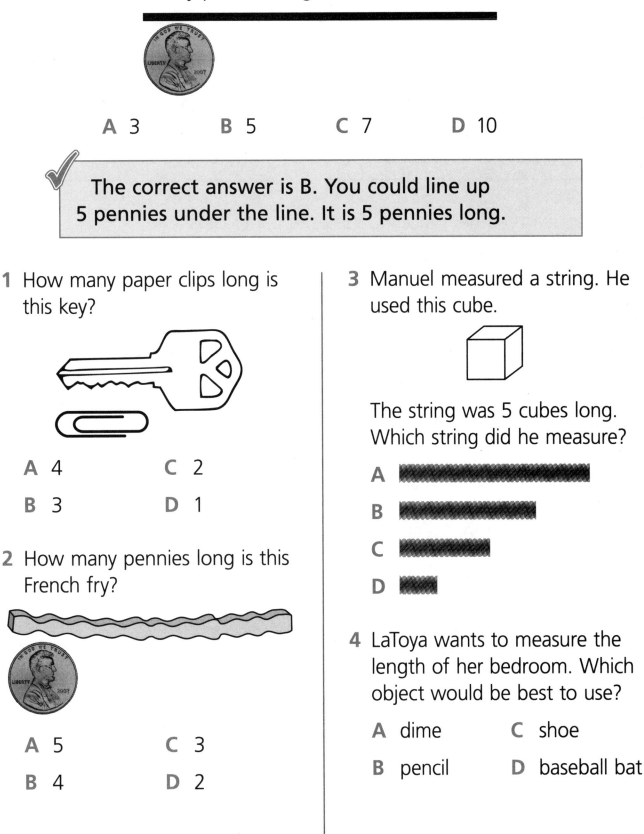

SAMPLE How many pennies long is this line?

A 3   B 5   C 7   D 10

✓ The correct answer is B. You could line up 5 pennies under the line. It is 5 pennies long.

1 How many paper clips long is this key?

A 4   C 2

B 3   D 1

2 How many pennies long is this French fry?

A 5   C 3

B 4   D 2

3 Manuel measured a string. He used this cube.

The string was 5 cubes long. Which string did he measure?

A
B
C
D

4 LaToya wants to measure the length of her bedroom. Which object would be best to use?

A dime   C shoe

B pencil   D baseball bat

© The Continental Press, Inc.   DUPLICATING THIS MATERIAL IS ILLEGAL.

SAMPLE Ali and Will measured the length of a sidewalk. They counted their footsteps. Ali counted 14 footsteps. Will counted 18 footsteps. Tell why this happened.

> ✓ Each boy counted his own footsteps. Ali counted fewer footsteps than Will. Ali took bigger footsteps. He did not need as many as Will.

5 Dana measured her bracelet. She used paper clips.

How many paper clips long is it?

Answer _____

6 Use a pencil to measure. How long is your desk?

Answer _____

7 Andy measured this pencil. He used coins.

Did Andy measure correctly? Tell how you know.

_____

_____

© The Continental Press, Inc. DUPLICATING THIS MATERIAL IS ILLEGAL.

8 Xun measured this straw. He used a penny.

Part A How many pennies long is the straw?

Answer _____

Part B Xun measured the straw again. He used this paper clip.

He thinks he will use the same number of paper clips as pennies. Is Xun correct? Tell how you know.

Look at the penny and the paper clip. Are they the same length?

_____

_____

_____

_____

UNIT 6
Measurement

103

© The Continental Press, Inc.   DUPLICATING THIS MATERIAL IS ILLEGAL.

Time

1.MD.3

There are 60 minutes in one hour. There are 30 minutes in a **half hour.**

You can write time with words.

3 o'clock

You can write time with numbers.

3:00

You can write half-hour times different ways.

Half past 3
Three thirty

These are both ways to write 3:30 with words.

This is a digital clock. It shows time with numbers.

Use a **clock** to tell time. A clock has two hands. The short hand is the **hour** hand. The long hand is the **minute** hand.

What time does this clock show?

Look at the short hand. It points to the hour: 3

Look at the long hand. It is pointing to the 12. This shows 0 minutes.

The time is 3 o'clock, or 3:00.

What time does this clock show?

Look at the short hand. It is between the 3 and the 4. The hour is 3.

Look at the long hand. It is pointing to the 6. The 6 is halfway around the clock. This shows 30 minutes.

The time is half past 3, or 3:30.

© The Continental Press, Inc.   DUPLICATING THIS MATERIAL IS ILLEGAL.

SAMPLE Which clock shows 7:30?

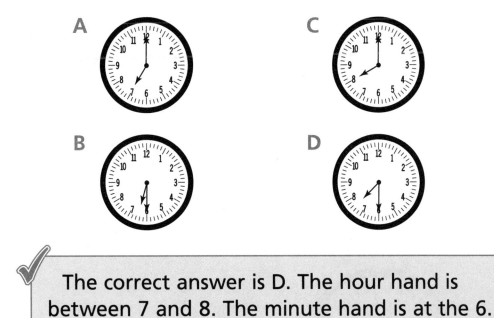

A

C

B

D

✓ The correct answer is D. The hour hand is between 7 and 8. The minute hand is at the 6.

1 Which clock shows nine o'clock?

A 8:00

C 9:30

B 9:00

D 10:00

2 What time does this clock show?

A 6:00

C 1:30

B 2:30

D 1:00

3 Which clock shows half past 4?

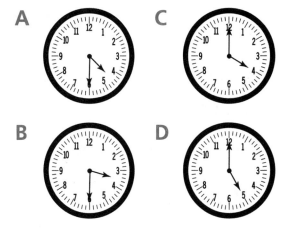

A

C

B

D

4 What time does this clock show?

A 12:30

C 11:30

B 12:00

D 11:00

© The Continental Press, Inc.   DUPLICATING THIS MATERIAL IS ILLEGAL.

SAMPLE Soccer practice starts at the time on this clock. What time does soccer practice start?

Answer _____

✓ Look at the minute hand. It points to the 12. There are 0 minutes. Look at the hour hand. It points to the 6. The time is 6:00.

5 Draw hands on this clock. Show 8:30.

6 School ends at the time on the clock.

What time does school end?

Answer _____

7 Write half past nine with numbers.

Answer _____

© The Continental Press, Inc.   DUPLICATING THIS MATERIAL IS ILLEGAL.

8 Mr. Warner went to see a movie. The movie started at half past ten.

Part A Draw hands on this clock. Show half past ten. Then write the time with numbers.

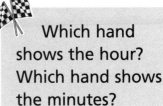

 Which hand shows the hour? Which hand shows the minutes?

Answer _____

Part B Mr. Warner looked at his watch when the movie ended.

Mr. Warner said the movie ended at 6 o'clock. Is Mr. Warner correct? Tell why or why not.

_____

_____

_____

_____

© The Continental Press, Inc.   DUPLICATING THIS MATERIAL IS ILLEGAL.

REVIEW

Measurement

Read each problem. Circle the letter of the best answer.

1 Look at this line.

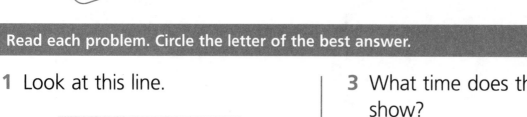

Which line is longer?

A ▬▬▬▬

B ▬▬▬▬▬

C ▬▬▬▬▬▬

D ▬▬▬▬▬▬▬

2 José measured this feather. He used a cube.

How many cubes long is the feather?

A 2   C 6

B 4   D 8

3 What time does this clock show?

A 1:00   C 11:00

B 10:00   D 12:00

4 Paula wants to measure the length of her finger. Which would be best to use?

A golf club

B pencil

C footstep

D penny

© The Continental Press, Inc.   DUPLICATING THIS MATERIAL IS ILLEGAL.

5 The Changs ate dinner at 5:30. Show 5:30 on this clock.

6 Quinn has this piece of string.

Draw a line that is shorter than Quinn's string. Draw it under the string.

7 How many pennies long is this hairbrush?

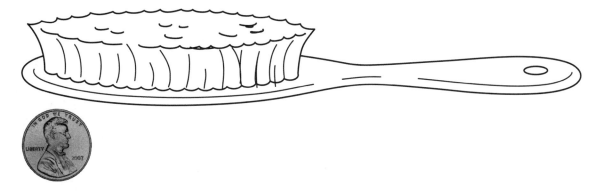

Answer _____

8 Write the time shown on this clock.

Answer _____

© The Continental Press, Inc.   DUPLICATING THIS MATERIAL IS ILLEGAL.

9 Three girls made strings of beads.

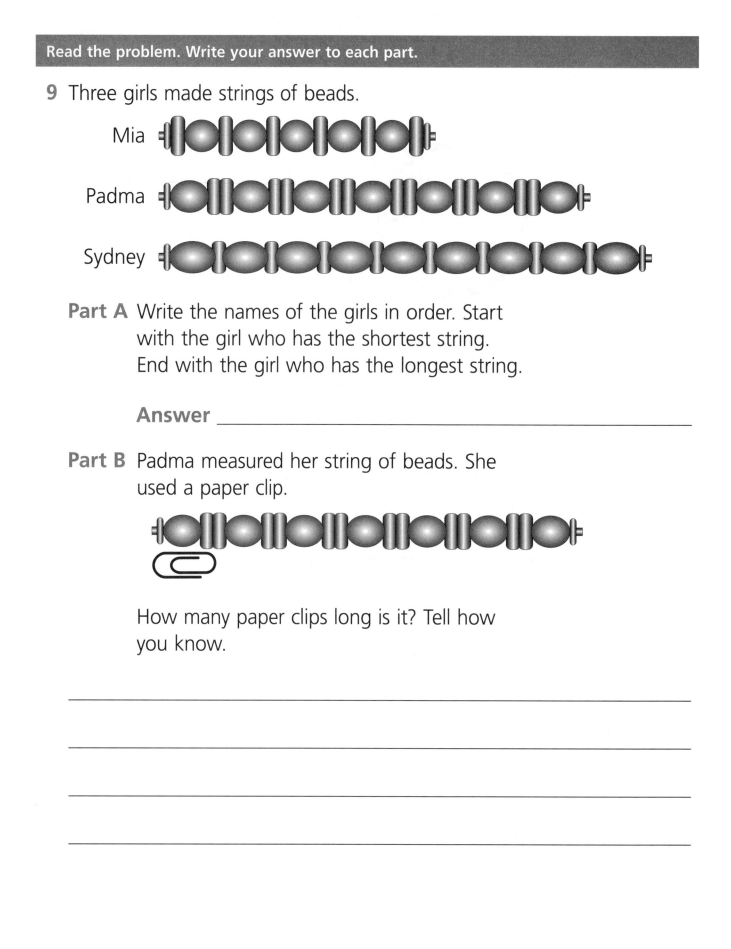

Mia

Padma

Sydney

Part A Write the names of the girls in order. Start with the girl who has the shortest string. End with the girl who has the longest string.

Answer _____

Part B Padma measured her string of beads. She used a paper clip.

How many paper clips long is it? Tell how you know.

_____

_____

_____

_____

© The Continental Press, Inc.   DUPLICATING THIS MATERIAL IS ILLEGAL.

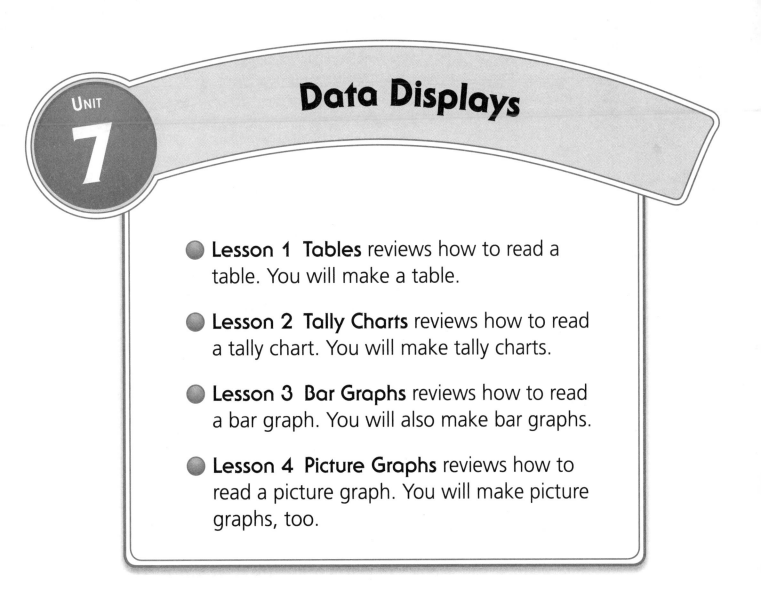

Data Displays

UNIT 7

- **Lesson 1 Tables** reviews how to read a table. You will make a table.

- **Lesson 2 Tally Charts** reviews how to read a tally chart. You will make tally charts.

- **Lesson 3 Bar Graphs** reviews how to read a bar graph. You will also make bar graphs.

- **Lesson 4 Picture Graphs** reviews how to read a picture graph. You will make picture graphs, too.

© The Continental Press, Inc.   DUPLICATING THIS MATERIAL IS ILLEGAL.

Tables

1.MD.4

Rows go across.

Columns go up and down.

You can use tables to answer many questions.

Read the question carefully. Find the information in the table.

Always read the title. It tells you what the table is about.

Read the labels. They tell you what is in the columns.

A **table** shows information. A table has **rows**. A table has **columns**.

How many children have a cat? Use the table.

PETS WE HAVE

Pet	Number of Children
Dog	4
Cat	9
Fish	3

Look at the "Pet" column. Find "Cat."
Look across from "Cat." Find how many: 9
There are 9 children with cats.

You can make a table.

Make a table to show the number of squares.

Write the colors in a column: green, white, black

Count the squares.
   Green: 4
   White: 6
   Black: 3
Write the numbers in the second column.

SQUARES

Color	Number
Green	4
White	6
Black	3

Give the graph a title.

© The Continental Press, Inc.   DUPLICATING THIS MATERIAL IS ILLEGAL.

SAMPLE Look at this table.

How many people picked vanilla?

A 4   C 15

B 8   D 27

FAVORITE ICE CREAM

Flavor	Number
Chocolate	15
Vanilla	8
Peanut Butter	4

✓ The correct answer is B. Find the row for vanilla. Read the number: 8. So 8 people picked vanilla.

Use the table above to answer questions 1 and 2.

1 How many more people picked chocolate than peanut butter?

A 10

B 11

C 15

D 19

2 Two more people picked chocolate. Now how many people picked chocolate?

A 13

B 15

C 17

D 20

3 Vicki has these marbles.

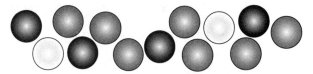

Which table shows her marbles?

A
Color	Number
Black	4
Green	7
White	2

B
Color	Number
Black	4
Green	2
White	7

C
Color	Number
Black	2
Green	4
White	7

D
Color	Number
Black	7
Green	4
White	2

© The Continental Press, Inc.   DUPLICATING THIS MATERIAL IS ILLEGAL.

SAMPLE Kevin has these toys. He made a table to show these toys.

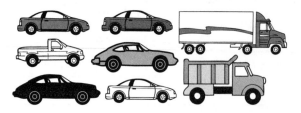

TOYS

Toy	Number
Car	3
Truck	5

What mistake did Kevin make?

Answer _____

> ✓ Kevin switched numbers in the table. He has 5 toy cars. He has 3 toy trucks. The table says he has 3 toy cars. It shows he has 5 toy trucks.

4 Some students picked their favorite sport.

Sport	Number
Soccer	
Football	
Baseball	

Make a table. Show this information. Give the table a title.

5 Use the table in question 4. How many students like soccer and football?

Answer _____

© The Continental Press, Inc.   DUPLICATING THIS MATERIAL IS ILLEGAL.

6 Look at this fruit.

Part A Make a table. Show the number of each kind of fruit. Give the table a title.

There are three kinds of fruit. There are apples. There are bananas. There are strawberries.

Fruit	Number

Part B Tell how you made your table.

_____

_____

_____

_____

© The Continental Press, Inc.   DUPLICATING THIS MATERIAL IS ILLEGAL.

Tally Charts

1.MD.4

A **tally** means 1 person or thing.

/ = 1

Tallies are grouped by 5's. The fifth tally goes across the first four.

/||| = 5

Count groups of tallies by 5's. Then count by 1's.

/||| /||| /||| //

Count: 5, 10, 15, 16, 17

A **tally chart** shows information. It looks like a table. It uses tallies instead of numbers.

How many children are playing tag?

PLAYGROUND GAMES

Game	Number Playing
Hide-and-seek	////
Tag	/||| /
Kickball	/||| /||| /

Find the row for "Tag."

Each tally shows one child. There is one group of 5 tallies. There is 1 more tally. Count: 5, 6

There are 6 children playing tag.

Make a tally chart. Always give the tally chart a title.

Make a tally chart. Show the number of shapes.

Count the circles: 8

Count the triangles: 4

Make one tally mark for each shape. Put the fifth mark across a group of four.

SHAPES

Shape	Number
Circle	/||| ///
Triangle	////

© The Continental Press, Inc. DUPLICATING THIS MATERIAL IS ILLEGAL.

SAMPLE Look at the tally chart.

How many books are on the shelf?

ITEMS ON SHELF

Item	Number
Book	//// //// //
DVD	//// /
Video Game	//// ////

A 2   C 10

B 7   D 12

The correct answer is D. Find the row for "Book."
Count the tallies: 5, 10, 11, 12. There are 12 books.

Use the tally chart above to answer questions 1 and 2.

1 How many video games are on the shelf?

A 4

B 6

C 9

D 10

2 How many items are on the shelf in all?

A 28

B 27

C 18

D 12

3 Addy has 3 stuffed cats. She has 10 bears and 5 dogs. Which tally chart shows this?

A

Animal	Number
Cat	///
Bear	////
Dog	//// ////

B

Animal	Number
Cat	///
Bear	//// /
Dog	//// / //// /

C

Animal	Number
Cat	////
Bear	//// ////
Dog	////

D

Animal	Number
Cat	///
Bear	//// ////
Dog	////

© The Continental Press, Inc.   DUPLICATING THIS MATERIAL IS ILLEGAL.

SAMPLE Jamal is making a tally chart. He has 14 pencils. Draw tallies to show 14.

Answer _____

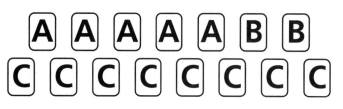

Put tallies in groups of 5's. Use 1 tally for each pencil. There will be two groups of 5. Then there will be 4 more tallies: *HH HH IIII*.

4 Some cards have letters on them.

A A A A A B B
C C C C C C C C

Make a tally chart to show this. Give the chart a title.

Letter	Number of Cards

5 There are 16 jump ropes. There are 12 hula hoops. Draw tallies to show these numbers.

Jump ropes _____

Hula hoops _____

© The Continental Press, Inc.   DUPLICATING THIS MATERIAL IS ILLEGAL.

6 A store has these hats for sale.

Part A Make a tally chart. Show the number of each color hat. Give the tally chart a title.

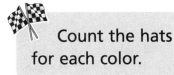
Count the hats for each color.

Color	Number of Hats

Part B Tell how you made the tally chart.

_____

_____

_____

_____

© The Continental Press, Inc.   DUPLICATING THIS MATERIAL IS ILLEGAL.

Bar Graphs

LESSON 3

1.MD.4

Read the labels on a bar graph. They help you understand the information.

The **scale** is the numbers on the side of the bar graph.

Sometimes the scale counts by 1's. It can count by 2's, 5's, or any other number.

A **bar graph** shows information. It uses bars to show how many.

Which class got the most votes?

Look for the tallest bar. This shows the most votes. The third bar is the tallest.

Read the label for this bar: Art

Art class got the most votes.

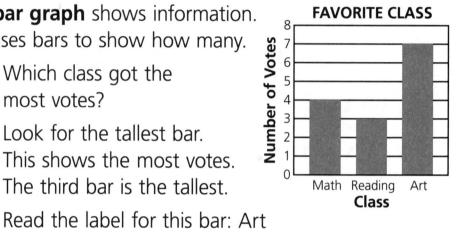

Make a bar graph. Draw bars to show numbers. Label the bar graph. Give it a title.

Make a bar graph. Show the information in the table.

FAVORITE COLOR

Color	Number
Red	6
Blue	8
Green	5

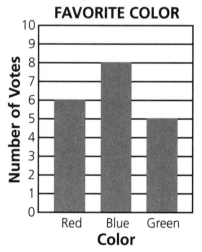

Write the colors at the bottom of the graph. Write numbers on the side of the graph. Draw bars to show the numbers. Give the graph a title.

© The Continental Press, Inc.   DUPLICATING THIS MATERIAL IS ILLEGAL.

SAMPLE Look at this bar graph.

How many oak trees are there?

A 2   C 5

B 4   D 6

TREES AT SCHOOL

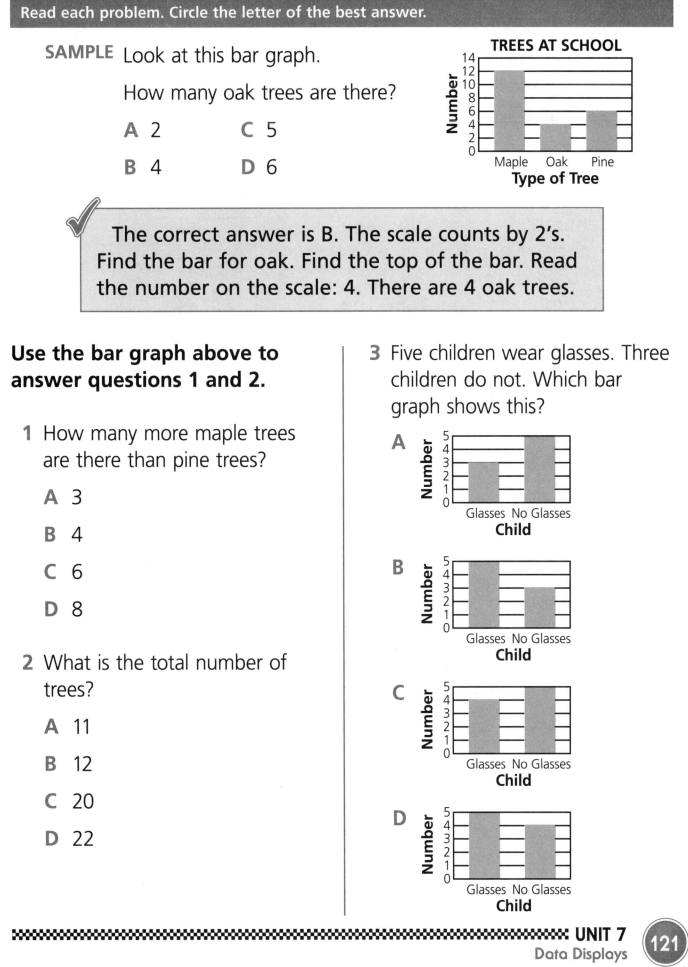

✓ The correct answer is B. The scale counts by 2's. Find the bar for oak. Find the top of the bar. Read the number on the scale: 4. There are 4 oak trees.

Use the bar graph above to answer questions 1 and 2.

1 How many more maple trees are there than pine trees?

A 3

B 4

C 6

D 8

2 What is the total number of trees?

A 11

B 12

C 20

D 22

3 Five children wear glasses. Three children do not. Which bar graph shows this?

A

B

C

D

© The Continental Press, Inc.   DUPLICATING THIS MATERIAL IS ILLEGAL.

SAMPLE Aaron has some coins in his pocket. He has 4 quarters. He has 2 dimes. He has 9 pennies. Make a bar graph to show this.

Write the names of the coins at the bottom. Write numbers at the side. Label the bar graph. Draw a bar for each coin. Show the number for that coin. The bar graph will look like this:

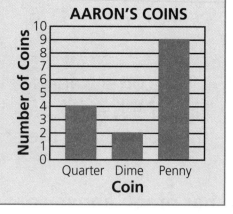

4 This table shows the prizes for an art contest.

Make a bar graph. Show this information.

ART CONTEST PRIZES

Prize	Number
Gold	5
Silver	8
Bronze	10

© The Continental Press, Inc.   DUPLICATING THIS MATERIAL IS ILLEGAL.

5 Look at the table. It shows some of the animals at a zoo.

ZOO ANIMALS

Animal	Number
Lion	5
Tiger	9
Giraffe	4

Part A Make a bar graph. Show the information in the table. Give the graph a title.

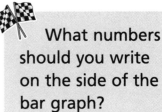

What numbers should you write on the side of the bar graph?

Part B The zoo got another lion. How would you change the bar graph?

_____

_____

_____

_____

© The Continental Press, Inc.   DUPLICATING THIS MATERIAL IS ILLEGAL.

Picture Graphs

1.MD.4

The **key** shows how many. Look at the key carefully.

A **picture graph** uses pictures to show how many.

How many shirts are there?

Look at the key. Each X is one piece of clothing.

CLOTHING IN SUITCASE

Clothing	Number
Pants	XX
Shirt	XXXX

Key: X = 1 piece

Find the row for shirts. Count the X's: 4

There are 4 shirts.

Make a picture graph.

Make a picture graph. Use the information in the table.

Think of a picture to use: ☥
Decide how many each picture shows: ☥ = 2 children

WAY TO SCHOOL

Way	Number
Bus	12
Walk	6
Drive	8

A picture can show 1, 2, or more things.

Give a picture graph a title. Label the columns.

Count by 2's to find the number of pictures:
    Bus: 2, 4, 6, 8, 10, 12
    Use 6 pictures.
    Walk: 2, 4, 6
    Use 3 pictures.
    Drive: 2, 4, 6, 8
    Use 4 pictures.

Make the pictograph.

WAY TO SCHOOL

Way	Number
Bus	☥ ☥ ☥ ☥ ☥ ☥
Walk	☥ ☥ ☥
Drive	☥ ☥ ☥ ☥

Key: ☥ = 2 children

© The Continental Press, Inc.   DUPLICATING THIS MATERIAL IS ILLEGAL.

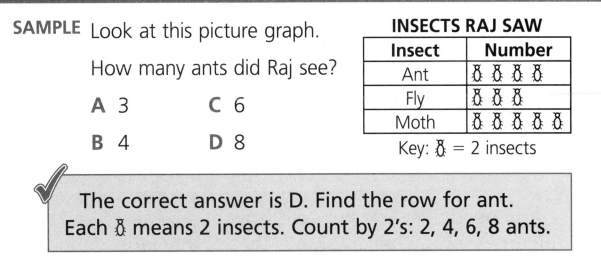

SAMPLE Look at this picture graph.

How many ants did Raj see?

A 3   C 6

B 4   D 8

INSECTS RAJ SAW

Insect	Number
Ant	🐜🐜🐜🐜
Fly	🐜🐜🐜
Moth	🐜🐜🐜🐜🐜

Key: 🐜 = 2 insects

✓ The correct answer is D. Find the row for ant.
Each 🐜 means 2 insects. Count by 2's: 2, 4, 6, 8 ants.

Use the picture graph above to answer questions 1 and 2.

1 Raj saw 14 beetles. He put this in his picture graph. Which row of pictures shows 14?

A 🐜🐜🐜🐜🐜🐜

B 🐜🐜🐜🐜🐜🐜🐜

C 🐜🐜🐜🐜🐜🐜🐜🐜🐜🐜

D 🐜🐜🐜🐜🐜🐜🐜🐜🐜🐜🐜🐜🐜

2 How many moths and flies did Raj see in all?

A 5

B 8

C 16

D 18

3 Which picture graph shows the information in this table?

DID YOU LIKE THE NEW MOVIE?

Answer	Number of People
Yes	7
No	5

A

Answer	Number
Yes	O O O
No	O O O

Key: O = 1 person

B

Answer	Number
Yes	O O O O O O O
No	O O O O O

Key: O = 1 person

C

Answer	Number
Yes	O O O O O
No	O O O O O O O

Key: O = 1 person

D

Answer	Number
Yes	O O O O
No	O O O

Key: O = 1 person

© The Continental Press, Inc.   DUPLICATING THIS MATERIAL IS ILLEGAL.

SAMPLE This is the key in a picture graph.

Key: 🍁 = 1 leaf

How many 🍁 do you need to show 9 leaves?

Answer _____

✓ You need 9 🍁. The key tells how many each picture shows. The key shows that 1 🍁 means 1 leaf. You need 9 🍁 to show 9 leaves.

Use this picture graph to answer questions 4 and 5.

4 How many black socks are there?

Answer _____

5 How many more white socks are there than blue socks?

Answer _____

SOCKS IN DRAWER

Color	Number of Socks
Blue	🧦🧦🧦🧦
Black	🧦🧦🧦🧦🧦🧦🧦
White	🧦🧦🧦🧦🧦

Key: 🧦 = 2 socks

---

6 Make a picture graph. Use the information in the table.

BIKES IN RACK

Color	Number of Bikes

Key: **X** = 1 bike

BIKES IN RACK

Color	Number
Red	2
Green	4
Black	3

UNIT 7 ▓▓▓▓▓▓▓▓▓▓▓▓▓▓▓▓▓▓▓▓▓▓▓▓▓▓▓▓▓▓
Data Displays

126

© The Continental Press, Inc.   DUPLICATING THIS MATERIAL IS ILLEGAL.

7 Some toys are in a toy box. There are 18 blocks. There are 4 dolls. There are 8 trucks.

Look at the key. Find how many each △ shows.

Part A Make a picture graph. Show the numbers of toys.

TOYS IN TOY BOX

Toy	Number of Toys

Key: △ = 2 toys

Part B Tell how you made your picture graph. Tell how you knew how many △ to use.

_____

_____

_____

_____

© The Continental Press, Inc.   DUPLICATING THIS MATERIAL IS ILLEGAL.

REVIEW

Data Displays

Read each problem. Circle the letter of the best answer.

1 Look at this tally chart.

FLOWERS IN VASE

Flower	Number
Daisy	///// ///// ///// /
Rose	///// ///
Lily	////

How many roses are in the vase?

A 4   **C** 8

B 7   **D** 16

2 A picture graph has this key.

Key: ☆ = 2 books

Which shows 16 books?

A ☆☆☆☆☆☆

B ☆☆☆☆☆ ☆☆☆

C ☆☆☆☆☆☆☆☆☆☆☆

D ☆☆☆☆☆☆☆☆☆☆☆☆☆☆☆☆

3 Look at these shapes.

○ □ □ ○ □ □ ○ □ □

Which table shows this?

A   **SHAPES**

Shape	Number
Circle	3
Square	5

B   **SHAPES**

Shape	Number
Circle	5
Square	3

C   **SHAPES**

Shape	Number
Circle	6
Square	3

D   **SHAPES**

Shape	Number
Circle	3
Square	6

© The Continental Press, Inc.   DUPLICATING THIS MATERIAL IS ILLEGAL.

Use the bar graph to answer questions 4 and 5.

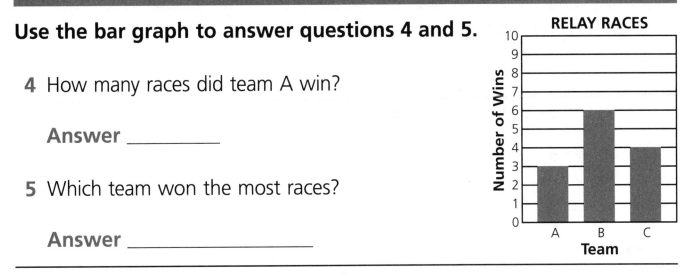

4 How many races did team A win?

Answer _____

5 Which team won the most races?

Answer _____

---

6 Gary and Tina found seashells. Gary found 9 seashells. Tina found 11 seashells. Make a picture graph to show this.

SEASHELLS

Person	Number of Seashells

Key: ⬡ = 1 seashell

7 Some children play a certain video game. Some do not.

DO YOU PLAY THIS VIDEO GAME?

Answer	Number of Children
Yes	15
No	7

How many children do **not** play the game?

Answer _____

© The Continental Press, Inc.   DUPLICATING THIS MATERIAL IS ILLEGAL.

8 A baker is baking loaves of bread. The tally chart shows the kinds of bread.

BREAD

Kind of Bread	Number of Loaves
White	//// //// //
Wheat	//// //
Raisin	////

Part A Make a bar graph. Show the information in the tally chart. Give the bar graph a title.

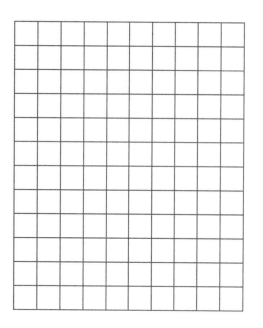

Part B Tell how you made the bar graph.

_____

_____

_____

© The Continental Press, Inc.   DUPLICATING THIS MATERIAL IS ILLEGAL.

Geometry

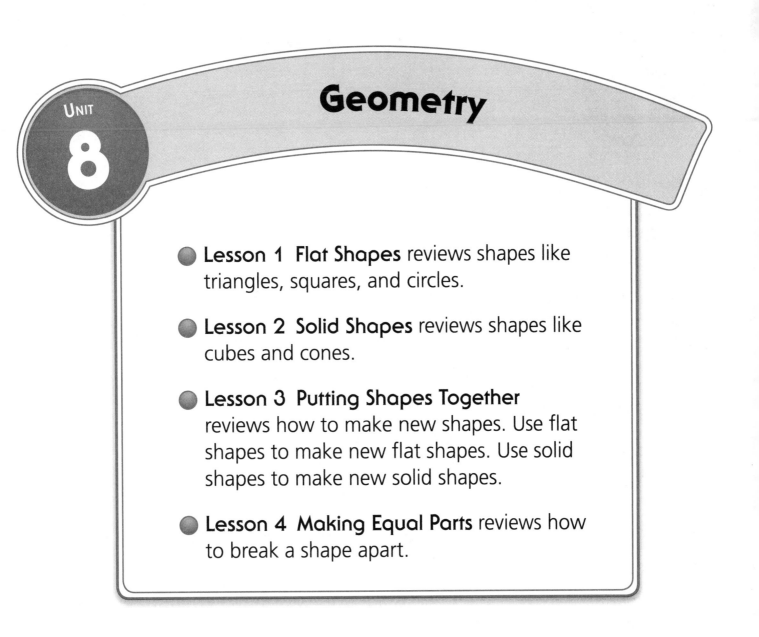

- **Lesson 1 Flat Shapes** reviews shapes like triangles, squares, and circles.

- **Lesson 2 Solid Shapes** reviews shapes like cubes and cones.

- **Lesson 3 Putting Shapes Together** reviews how to make new shapes. Use flat shapes to make new flat shapes. Use solid shapes to make new solid shapes.

- **Lesson 4 Making Equal Parts** reviews how to break a shape apart.

© The Continental Press, Inc.   DUPLICATING THIS MATERIAL IS ILLEGAL.

Flat Shapes

1.G.1

A **side** is straight. A **corner** is where two sides meet.

A circle is round. It does not have sides or corners.

The number of sides on a flat shape does not change. The number of corners does not change.

The color of a shape can change. The size of a shape can change. The position of a shape can change.

Some flat shapes have sides and corners. Some are round.

Rectangle   Square   Trapezoid   Triangle   Circle

Some things are always true about a flat shape.

Emily drew a flat shape. It had 3 sides. What kind of shape did she draw?

Look for clues.
  1. It is a flat shape.
  2. It has 3 sides.

A flat shape with 3 sides is a triangle. So Emily drew a triangle.

Some things are not always true about a flat shape.

Roger drew a flat shape. He colored it green. What kind of shape did he draw?

Look for clues.
  1. It is a flat shape.
  2. It is green.

You cannot tell what kind of shape it is. He could have drawn a green rectangle. Or he could have drawn a green circle. You cannot answer the question.

© The Continental Press, Inc.   DUPLICATING THIS MATERIAL IS ILLEGAL.

SAMPLE Nick drew a flat shape. It has 4 sides and 4 corners. Which of these is **not** Nick's shape?

A square   B trapezoid C circle   D rectangle

✓ The correct answer is C. A square has 4 sides and 4 corners. A trapezoid and a rectangle do, too. A circle does not have any sides. It is round. Nick might have drawn a square, a trapezoid, or a rectangle. He did not draw a circle.

1 Mr. Garcia drew a square on the board. What is always true about a square?

A It is purple.

B It has 4 sides.

C It is on the board.

D It is very big.

2 What is the name of this flat shape?

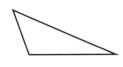

A triangle   C circle

B square   D trapezoid

3 Shelby must pick a flat shape. She has these clues.

   1. It has no corners.
   2. It is black.

Can Shelby name the flat shape?

A No, she needs to know the number of sides.

B No, she needs to know how big it is.

C Yes, she knows it is black.

D Yes, she knows the number of corners.

4 Which of these is a rectangle?

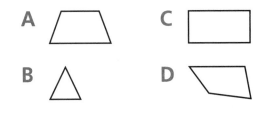

© The Continental Press, Inc.   DUPLICATING THIS MATERIAL IS ILLEGAL.

SAMPLE Kara must draw a flat shape. She knows it is yellow. She knows one side is longer than her pencil. Can she draw the shape? Tell why or why not.

> ✓ **No, she cannot draw the shape. She needs to know how many sides it has. She could draw a triangle that is yellow. She could draw a rectangle that is yellow. But they are different shapes.**

5 Draw a flat shape at the right. The shape has 4 sides and 4 corners. All the sides are the same length. The corners are square. Name the shape.

Answer _____

6 Cesar drew one of these shapes.

A   B   C   D

Cesar said, "My flat shape is green." Can you tell which shape Cesar drew? Tell why or why not.

_____

_____

_____

7 How many sides does a trapezoid have?

Answer _____

© The Continental Press, Inc.   DUPLICATING THIS MATERIAL IS ILLEGAL.

8 Ms. Fisher told her class to draw a flat shape. She said the shape must have 3 sides.

Part A Draw this flat shape in the space below.

Part B Matsu and Caleb both listened to Ms. Fisher. They drew these shapes.

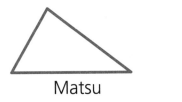

Matsu   Caleb

Who drew the right shape? Tell how you know.

What is always true about this shape? What is *not* always true about this shape?

_____

_____

_____

_____

© The Continental Press, Inc.   DUPLICATING THIS MATERIAL IS ILLEGAL.

Solid Shapes

1.G.1

A **sphere** is a round solid shape. It looks like a ball.

A **face** is a side of a solid shape. It is always a flat shape.

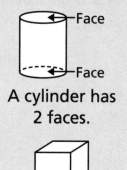

A cylinder has 2 faces.

A cube has 6 faces.

Solid shapes are not flat. Some solids have flat sides. Some can roll.

Cone   Cylinder   Cube   Rectangular prism

Look at the things you use everyday. There are many that are shaped like solid shapes.

What is this solid shape?

Soup

Look at the soup can. It is round. The top is a circle. The bottom is a circle, too.

Look for a shape that is the same: cylinder

The soup can is a cylinder.

© The Continental Press, Inc.   DUPLICATING THIS MATERIAL IS ILLEGAL.

SAMPLE What part of this shape **cannot** change?

A the color

C the shape of the faces

B the size

D the place it is sitting

> The correct answer is C. The solid shape is a cube. A cube can be a different color. It can be bigger or smaller. It can be sitting on a table or on the floor. It will still be a cube. It must have squares as the faces. You cannot change the shape of the faces.

1 Which has the same shape as a cone?

A   **C**

B   **D**

2 What is the name of this shape?

A cone

B cylinder

C cube

D rectangular prism

3 Bob uses paper to make a cylinder. Which of these is **not** Bob's shape?

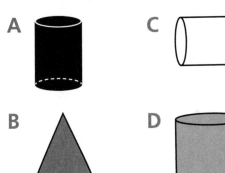

A   **C**

B   **D**

4 Which of these is a solid shape that can roll?

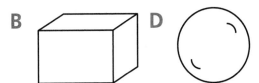

A   **C**

B   **D**

© The Continental Press, Inc.   DUPLICATING THIS MATERIAL IS ILLEGAL.

SAMPLE Tanner made a solid figure. It can roll. It has a point at the top. What is the solid figure?

Answer _____

Tanner made a cone. A cone has a circle for a face. So it is round. It can roll. It has a point at the top. A cone looks like this: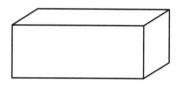

5 Petra made this solid figure.

She wants to make another solid figure like this. She wants to change something. Name a part of the solid figure that she can change.

Answer _____

6 Look at the figures below. Color in the cylinders.

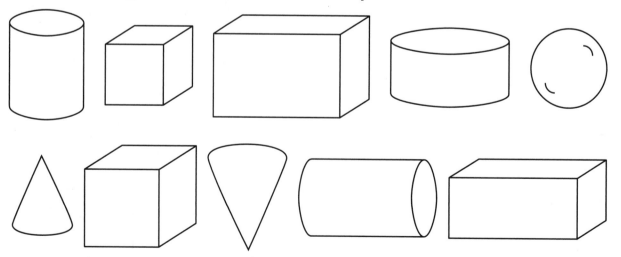

© The Continental Press, Inc.   DUPLICATING THIS MATERIAL IS ILLEGAL.

7 Evan has these toy blocks.

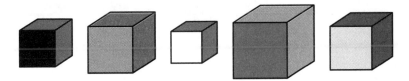

Part A Evan says the toy blocks are the same solid figure. Is Evan right? Tell why or why not.

What is the same about these solid figures? What is different about them?

_____

_____

_____

_____

Part B Evan also has these toy blocks.

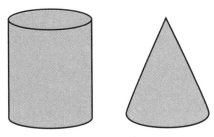

Are these two solid figures the same? Tell how you know.

_____

_____

_____

_____

© The Continental Press, Inc. DUPLICATING THIS MATERIAL IS ILLEGAL.

Putting Shapes Together

1.G.2

Sometimes you can make more than one shape. You can put the shapes together in different ways.

You can put different shapes together.

This figure is made of a rectangle and a square.

Put flat figures together along the sides.

Put solid figures together at their faces.

You can use parts of a circle.

Half circle

Quarter circle

You can put flat shapes together. You can make new shapes.

Bryan has these flat shapes. He puts them together. What shape could he make?

He could make a trapezoid:

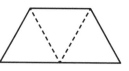

You can put solid shapes together to make new shapes.

Greta has two cubes. She puts them together. What shape can she make?

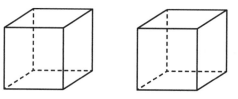

Greta can make a rectangular prism:

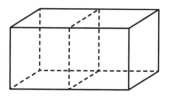

© The Continental Press, Inc.   DUPLICATING THIS MATERIAL IS ILLEGAL.

SAMPLE Which shape could you make with these flat shapes?

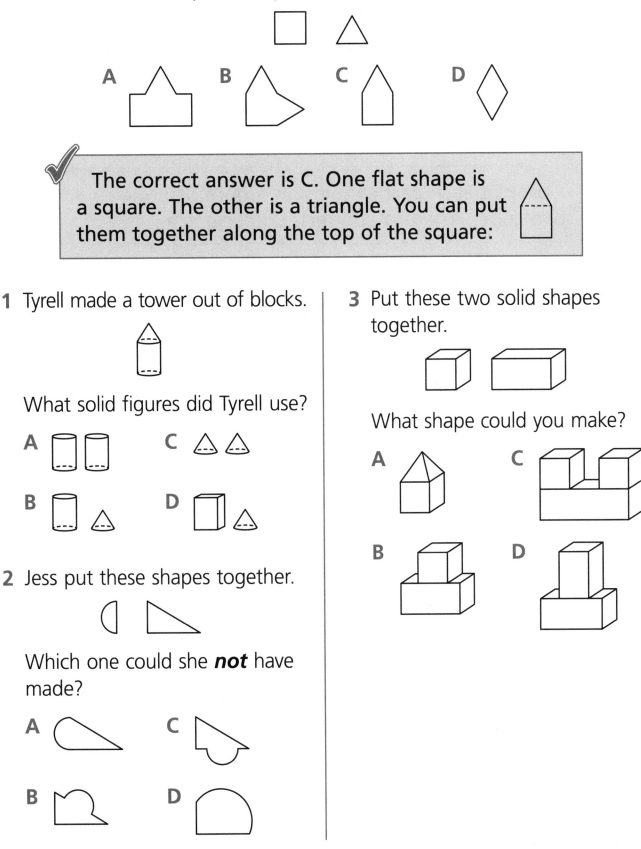

The correct answer is C. One flat shape is a square. The other is a triangle. You can put them together along the top of the square:

1 Tyrell made a tower out of blocks.

What solid figures did Tyrell use?

A   C

B   D

2 Jess put these shapes together.

Which one could she **not** have made?

A   C

B   D

3 Put these two solid shapes together.

What shape could you make?

A   C

B   D

© The Continental Press, Inc.   DUPLICATING THIS MATERIAL IS ILLEGAL.

SAMPLE Luis used three solid shapes. He made a new shape.

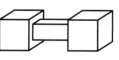

What solid shapes did Luis use?

Answer _____

✓ **Look at each part of the solid figure. There are two cubes. There is one rectangular prism.**

4 Look at these three flat shapes.

Put these shapes together. Make a new shape. Draw it in the space below.

5 Look at the flat shapes below.

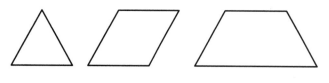

Put these shapes together. Make this shape: ⬡.

© The Continental Press, Inc. DUPLICATING THIS MATERIAL IS ILLEGAL.

6 April cut some flat shapes out of paper.

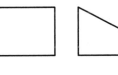

Part A April taped the shapes together. She made a 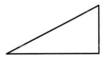 new shape. Draw a new shape in the space below.

> You can turn the flat shapes. You can move them, too.

Part B April says there is more than one way to put the shapes together. Make another new shape. Draw it in the space below.

Tell how you made your new shape.

_____

_____

_____

_____

© The Continental Press, Inc.   DUPLICATING THIS MATERIAL IS ILLEGAL.

Making Equal Parts

1.G.3

Use these words for two equal parts:

Half

One-half

Half of

Halves is the plural of *half*.

Use these words for four equal parts:

Fourth

Quarter

One-fourth

One-quarter

Fourth of

Quarter of

Divide a shape to make equal parts. Equal parts are the same size.

Divide this circle. Make two equal parts.

Draw a line down the middle. The part on the left is the same as the part on the right.

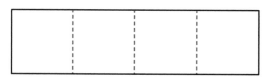

There are two equal parts. Each part is half of the circle.

This rectangle was split into equal parts. How many equal parts are in the whole rectangle?

Count the equal parts: 4

You can say the rectangle is divided into fourths.

© The Continental Press, Inc. DUPLICATING THIS MATERIAL IS ILLEGAL.

SAMPLE Look at this rectangle.

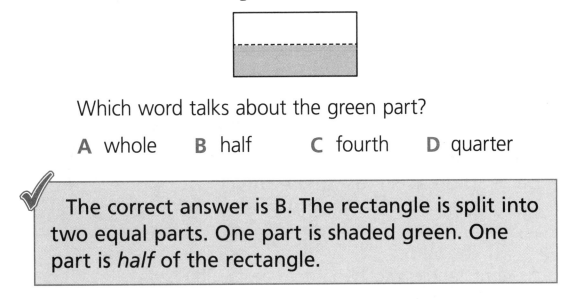

Which word talks about the green part?

A whole   **B** half   **C** fourth   **D** quarter

✓ The correct answer is B. The rectangle is split into two equal parts. One part is shaded green. One part is *half* of the rectangle.

1 Which circle shows quarters?

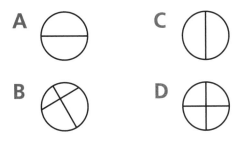

2 Tristan cut a rectangle into four equal pieces. He colored one piece red. What word talks about the red piece?

A half   **C** fourth

B some   **D** whole

3 Krista has these pieces.

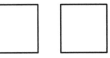

She puts them together. She makes a rectangle. How many equal parts did she use to make the rectangle?

A 2   **C** 4

B 3   **D** 6

4 Luca colored one half of a circle. Which circle shows this?

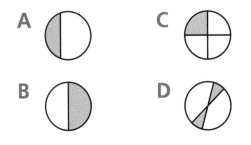

© The Continental Press, Inc.   DUPLICATING THIS MATERIAL IS ILLEGAL.

SAMPLE Divide this circle into fourths.

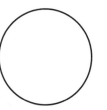

✓ *Fourths* means four equal shares. Draw lines on the circle. Make four parts. The parts must all be the same size.

5 Maria cut a rectangle into two equal parts. She gave one part to her sister. She kept one part. What part of the rectangle did Maria keep?

Answer _____

6 Divide this rectangle into quarters. Shade one quarter.

7 Look at this piece of a circle.

How many pieces do you need to make a whole circle?

Answer _____

UNIT 8 ▨▨▨▨▨▨▨▨▨▨▨▨▨▨▨▨▨▨▨▨▨▨▨▨▨▨▨▨▨▨
Geometry

© The Continental Press, Inc. DUPLICATING THIS MATERIAL IS ILLEGAL.

8 Look at these two circles.

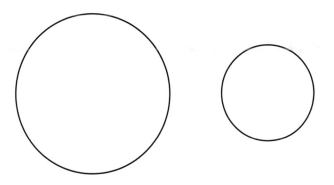

Part A Divide both circles into fourths. Shade one fourth in each circle.

Part B Look at the shaded parts of both circles. Are they the same size? Tell why or why not.

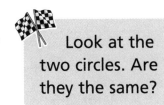

Look at the two circles. Are they the same?

_____

_____

_____

_____

© The Continental Press, Inc.   DUPLICATING THIS MATERIAL IS ILLEGAL.

REVIEW

Geometry

Read each problem. Circle the letter of the best answer.

1 What is the name of this flat shape?

A triangle   C square

B circle   D rectangle

2 Put these solid shapes together.

What shape could you make?

A

C

B

D

3 Look at this solid shape.

What part of this shape **cannot** change?

A the color

B the size

C the place it is sitting

D the number of faces

4 Which rectangle shows quarters?

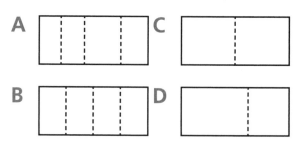

5 Which flat shape does **not** have 4 sides?

A triangle   C square

B rectangle   D trapezoid

© The Continental Press, Inc.   DUPLICATING THIS MATERIAL IS ILLEGAL.

6 Look at these flat shapes.

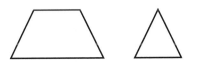

Put these shapes together. Make a new shape. Draw the new shape at the right.

7 Split this circle into halves.

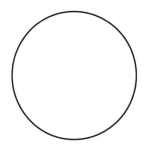

8 Which flat shape does **not** have any sides or corners?

Answer _____

9 Look at the solid shapes below. Color in the cubes.

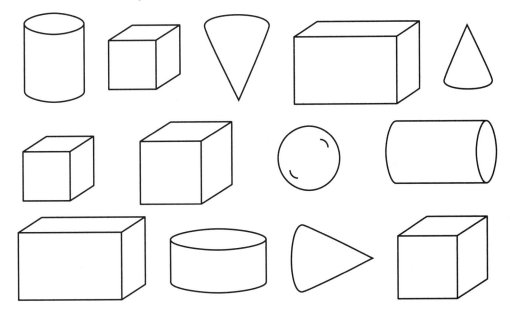

© The Continental Press, Inc.   DUPLICATING THIS MATERIAL IS ILLEGAL.

10 Dean cut three flat shapes out of paper.

1. This shape had 3 sides.

2. This shape had 4 sides. All the sides were the same length. The corners are square.

3. This shape had 4 sides. The sides across from each other were the same length. The corners are square.

Part A Draw these shapes in the space below. Label them 1, 2, and 3.

Part B Dean taped the shapes together. He made a new shape. Make a new shape. Draw it in the space below.

© The Continental Press, Inc.   DUPLICATING THIS MATERIAL IS ILLEGAL.

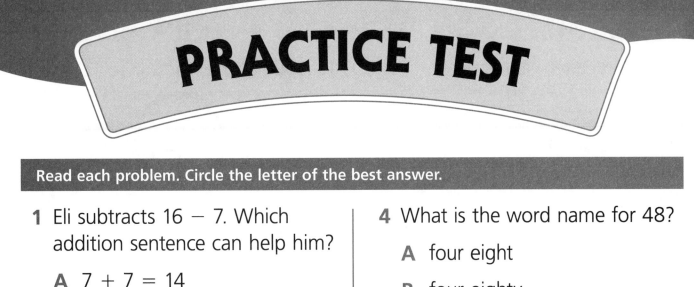

PRACTICE TEST

1 Eli subtracts $16 - 7$. Which addition sentence can help him?

  A $7 + 7 = 14$

  B $7 + 8 = 15$

  C $9 + 7 = 16$

  D $8 + 8 = 16$

2 Which of these is correct?

  A $62 < 72$

  B $58 < 51$

  C $35 > 37$

  D $26 > 62$

3 Which is the same as $5 + 2$?

  A $2 + 2$

  B $2 + 5$

  C $5 + 5$

  D $2 + 5 + 2$

4 What is the word name for 48?

  A four eight

  B four-eighty

  C forty-eight

  D four and eight

5 Look at this golf club.

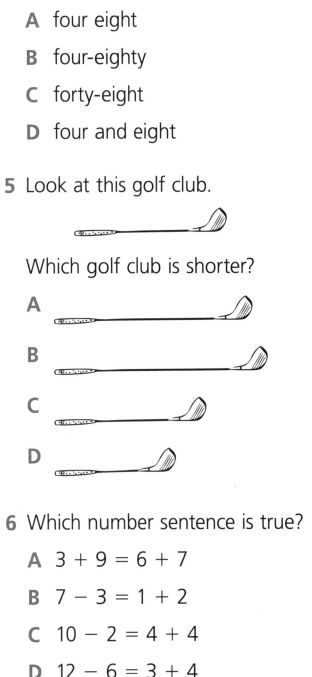

Which golf club is shorter?

  A

  B

  C

  D

6 Which number sentence is true?

  A $3 + 9 = 6 + 7$

  B $7 - 3 = 1 + 2$

  C $10 - 2 = 4 + 4$

  D $12 - 6 = 3 + 4$

© The Continental Press, Inc.   DUPLICATING THIS MATERIAL IS ILLEGAL.

7 Subtract: 80
                  −30

   A 40

   B 50

   C 60

   D 70

8 Omar had 7 pennies. Kasey had 4 pennies. Jane had 6 pennies. How many pennies did they have in all?

   A 17

   B 16

   C 11

   D 10

9 Look at this number line.

0 1 2 3 4 5 6 7 8 9 10

Start at 6. Count back 2. What number is this?

   A 2

   B 3

   C 4

   D 5

10 Look at the clock.

What time is it?

   A 4:00

   B 4:30

   C 5:00

   D 5:30

11 Look at the model below.

What number does the model show?

   A 10

   B 14

   C 41

   D 104

© The Continental Press, Inc.   DUPLICATING THIS MATERIAL IS ILLEGAL.

12 Add:

$$56 + 8$$

A 54

B 62

C 64

D 66

13 Find the sum.

$$3 + 8 + 2 = \square$$

A 10

B 11

C 12

D 13

14 A flat shape has 4 sides. The sides are all the same length. What is the flat shape?

A rectangle

B square

C circle

D trapezoid

15 Look at this ten frame.

What addition sentence does it show?

A $7 + 3 = 10$

B $7 + 8 = 15$

C $7 + 9 = 16$

D $8 + 8 = 16$

16 Which rectangle shows halves?

© The Continental Press, Inc.   DUPLICATING THIS MATERIAL IS ILLEGAL.

17 Look at this table.

FLAG COLORS

Color	Number of Flags
Blue	14
Green	18
Red	12

How many green flags are there?

A 12   C 18

B 14   D 30

18 Heather starts at 24. She counts on 5. What numbers does she say?

A 24, 25, 26, 27, 28

B 25, 26, 27, 28, 29

C 24, 25, 26, 27, 28, 29

D 23, 22, 21, 20, 19

19 How long is this comb?

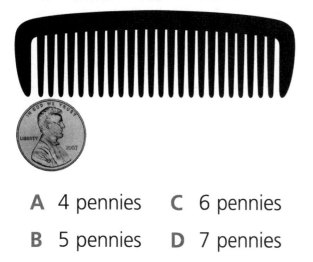

A 4 pennies   C 6 pennies

B 5 pennies   D 7 pennies

20 Which clock shows 7:00?

A
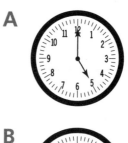

B

C

D

21 Which number is 3 tens and 0 ones?

A 03

B 13

C 30

D 300

© The Continental Press, Inc.   DUPLICATING THIS MATERIAL IS ILLEGAL.

22 Sam has these blocks.

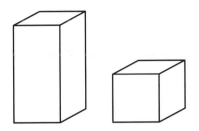

Sam puts the blocks together. Which figure could he make?

A

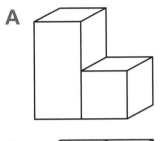

B

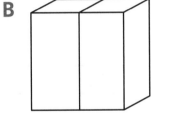

C

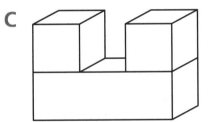

D

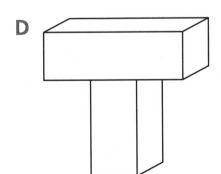

23 Find the sum.

$$48 + 20 = \square$$

A 60

B 68

C 70

D 78

24 A solid figure has two faces. They are both circles. What solid figure is this?

A cone

B sphere

C cube

D cylinder

25 Anton wants to subtract 19 − 8. What addition sentence can Anton use?

A $19 + \square = 8$

B $19 + 8 = \square$

C $8 + \square = 19$

D $8 + 19 = \square$

© The Continental Press, Inc.   DUPLICATING THIS MATERIAL IS ILLEGAL.

26 Which of these does **not** show a ten?

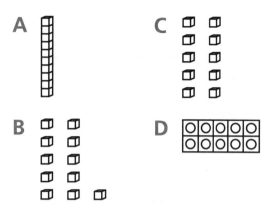

A | C

B | D

27 Carrie made 15 cookies. She gave 8 of them away. How many cookies are left?

A 7   C 5

B 6   D 4

28 What number is missing?

$$\square + 12 = 18$$

A 30   C 6

B 20   D 5

29 What is 10 more than 71?

A 61   C 80

B 70   D 81

30 Look at these jacks.

Which tally chart shows the jacks correctly?

A   JACKS

Color	Number
Green	//// ////
White	//// //// ////
Black	//// /

B   JACKS

Color	Number
Green	/////////
White	/////////////
Black	/////

C   JACKS

Color	Number
Green	////
White	//// ///
Black	//// //// //

D   JACKS

Color	Number
Green	//// ///
White	//// //// //
Black	////

Practice Test

© The Continental Press, Inc.   DUPLICATING THIS MATERIAL IS ILLEGAL.

31 Add. Show your work.

$$
\begin{array}{r}
27 \\
+34 \\
\hline
\end{array}
$$

Answer _____

32 Lacey wants to subtract 14 − 8. She breaks 8 apart to make it easier. Tell what she did.

_____

_____

33 Nikki ate breakfast at 8:30. Draw hands on the clock. Show 8:30.

34 Look at this number line.

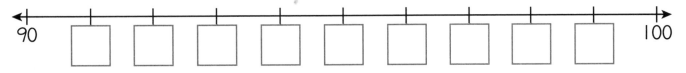

Fill in the numbers on the number line.

© The Continental Press, Inc.   DUPLICATING THIS MATERIAL IS ILLEGAL.

35 Marco cut these shapes out of paper.

Marco put the shapes together. He made a new shape. Draw a new shape in the space below.

36 Look at these three ribbons.

Green
Black
White

Put these ribbons in order. Start with the longest ribbon. End with the shortest ribbon.

Answer _____

37 Break this circle into fourths.

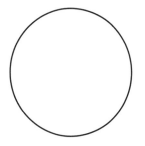

© The Continental Press, Inc.   **DUPLICATING THIS MATERIAL IS ILLEGAL.**

38 Look at this number sentence.

$$12 + 5 = 19 - 2$$

Is it true? Tell how you know.

_____

_____

39 Look at these number blocks.

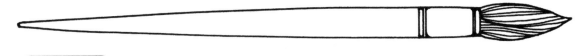

What number do the blocks show?

Answer _____

40 Gina found the length of this paintbrush. She used paper clips.

How many paper clips long is the paintbrush?

Answer _____

41 What is 10 less than 98?

Answer _____

© The Continental Press, Inc.   DUPLICATING THIS MATERIAL IS ILLEGAL.

42 Make a bar graph. Show the information in the table. Give the graph a title.

TYPES OF BIRDS

Bird	Number
Robin	8
Blue jay	2
Crow	4

43 Mr. Turner put some books in boxes.

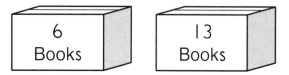

6 Books   13 Books

How many books does he have in all? Show your work.

Answer _____

44 Compare these numbers. Use <, >, or =.

45 ☐ 38

© The Continental Press, Inc.   DUPLICATING THIS MATERIAL IS ILLEGAL.

45 Find the missing number. Tell how you found the
number.

$$15 = \square - 3$$

_____

_____

46 Neil drew these two flat shapes.

Are they the same flat shape? Tell how you know.

_____

_____

47 Look at this number.

17

Write the number of tens. Write the number of
ones.

Tens _____

Ones _____

© The Continental Press, Inc.   DUPLICATING THIS MATERIAL IS ILLEGAL.

48 Peter made a picture graph. He showed the number of photos he took each day. He used this key.

Key: $\boxed{\cdot \text{O}}$ = 2 photos

One day, he took 6 photos. He puts this in the picture graph. How many $\boxed{\cdot \text{O}}$ does he need to use?

Answer _____

49 Use the number line. Start at 11. Count on 4. What numbers do you say?

Answer _____

50 There were three fishbowls. The first bowl had 3 fish. The second bowl had 7 fish. The third bowl had 6 fish.

How many fish were there in all?

Answer _____

© The Continental Press, Inc.   DUPLICATING THIS MATERIAL IS ILLEGAL.

51 Lindsey adds 7 + 6.

Part A Use this ten frame to add 7 + 6. Write the sum.

Answer _____

Part B Look at the addition fact in part A. What are two related subtraction facts?

Answer _____

© The Continental Press, Inc.   DUPLICATING THIS MATERIAL IS ILLEGAL.

52 Three friends practiced basketball. They made this tally chart.

BASKETBALL PRACTICE

Friend	Number of Baskets Made
Joe	⫽⫽⫽⫽ ⫽⫽⫽⫽ ⫽⫽⫽⫽
Hisoka	⫽⫽⫽⫽ ⫽⫽⫽
Cody	⫽⫽⫽⫽ ⫽⫽⫽⫽

Part A How many more baskets did Joe make than Cody?

Answer _____

Part B Make a picture graph. Show the information in the tally chart. Give the graph a title.

Friend	Number of Baskets Made

Key: ⊕ = 2 baskets

© The Continental Press, Inc.   DUPLICATING THIS MATERIAL IS ILLEGAL.

53 Teri had these ones blocks. She put some together. She made a ten.

Part A Circle how many Teri put together. Write the number all of the blocks above show.

Answer _____

Part B Teri uses number blocks to show 80. How many tens rods does she need? How many ones blocks does she need? Tell how you know.

_____

_____

_____

_____

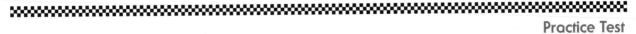

© The Continental Press, Inc.   DUPLICATING THIS MATERIAL IS ILLEGAL.

GLOSSARY

A   **add**   to put groups together

B   **bar graph**   a data display that uses bars to show information

C   **circle**   a flat shape with no sides or corners. It is round.

      clock   a tool used to tell time

      column   part of a table that goes up and down

      compare   to decide which number is greater or less; to decide which length is shorter or longer

      cone   a solid shape with 1 face. The face is a circle. The curved part meets at a point.

      corner   where two sides meet on a flat shape

      count   to say numbers in order to find how many

© The Continental Press, Inc.   DUPLICATING THIS MATERIAL IS ILLEGAL.

cube	a solid shape with 6 faces. The faces are squares.	
cylinder	a solid shape with 2 faces. The faces are circles. It has a curved part, too.	

D **digit** a numeral from 0 to 9: 0, 1, 2, 3, 4, 5, 6, 7, 8, 9

doubles facts an addition sentence that adds the same number to itself; Example: 4 + 4 = 8

E **equal** is the same as

equal parts pieces of a shape that are the same size

equal sign shows that numbers are the same (=)

F **face** the side of a solid shape. It is always a flat shape.

fact family set of four related facts that use the same three numbers

G **greater** describes a number that is more

© The Continental Press, Inc.   DUPLICATING THIS MATERIAL IS ILLEGAL.

(H) **half hour**   30 minutes

hour   a unit of time. There are 24 hours in 1 day. There are 60 minutes in 1 hour.

(K) **key**   the part of a picture graph that tells how many each picture shows

(L) **length**   how long, tall, or wide something is

less   describes a number that is smaller

(M) **measure**   to find how long something is

minus sign   shows subtraction (−)

minute   a unit of time. There are 60 minutes in 1 hour.

(N) **numbers**   words and signs to show how many

number line   a line showing numbers in order

number sentence   shows a relationship with numbers and symbols; Example: 2 + 3 = 5

number stories   a problem that uses words to tell about something and ask a question. You must decide how to answer it.

© The Continental Press, Inc.   DUPLICATING THIS MATERIAL IS ILLEGAL.

O — **ones** — the first place on the right in a number; Example: in 25, the 5 is in the ones place.

P — **picture graph** — a data display that uses pictures to show how many

place value — the value of a digit in a number

Tens	Ones
5	7

plus sign — shows addition (+)

R — **rectangle** — a flat shape with 4 sides and 4 corners. The opposite sides are the same length. The corners are square.

rectangular prism — a solid shape with 6 faces that are rectangles

regroup — to change 10 ones to 1 ten, or to change 1 ten to 10 ones

row — part of a table that goes across

S — **scale** — the numbers on a bar graph

side — the straight part of a flat shape

© The Continental Press, Inc. DUPLICATING THIS MATERIAL IS ILLEGAL.

solve	to find the answer to a math problem; to find the missing number in a number sentence
sphere	a solid shape that is round, like a ball
square	a flat shape with 4 sides and 4 corners. The sides are all the same length. The corners are square.
subtract	to take a group apart
symbol	something that stands for a word or phrase
table	data display with rows and columns
tally	a slash that shows 1 person or thing in a tally chart (/), grouped in 5's with the fifth tally across the first four (////)
tally chart	a table that uses tallies to show information
tens	the second place from the right in a number; Example: in 25, the 2 is in the tens place.
trapezoid	a flat shape with 4 sides and 4 corners. Two sides are always the same distance apart.
triangle	a flat shape with 3 sides and 3 corners

© The Continental Press, Inc. DUPLICATING THIS MATERIAL IS ILLEGAL.